The I'd-Rather-Be-Quilting Cookbook

The I'd-Rather-Be-Quilting-Cookbook

MIRIAM LAYTON

PATRICIA A. WALKER

MARION WILLIAMS

Madrona Publishers • *Seattle* • 1982

Published by
Madrona Publishers, Inc.
2116 Western Avenue
Seattle, Washington 98121

FIRST EDITION
10 9 8 7 6 5 4 3 2

Library of Congress Cataloging in Publication Data

Layton, Miriam, 1908–
    The I'd rather be quilting cookbook.

    Includes index.
    1. Cookery. 2. Quilting—Patterns. I. Walker, Patricia A., 1928– .
II. Williams, Marion, 1932– . III. Title.
TX715.L38   641.5   82–7152
ISBN 0-914842-86-2   AACR2

Drawings by Edwin T. Layton, U.S.N. Adm. (ret.)

ACKNOWLEDGEMENTS

    We wish to acknowledge and thank our families and friends for
their valuable help, especially Jan Allnutt, Joan Bergsund, Marilyn
Bragdon, Nancy Kelly, Edwin Layton, Marcia Macklin, Dorothea
Walker Shuster, Phyllis Smith, George Walker and Bill Williams.

To EDWIN, GEORGE, *and* BILL
for their support and love.

Preface

It all started with Beginning Quilting. We each thought how nice it would be to make a patchwork pillow or two for our friends and maybe a quilt for our own beds. Pretty soon we found ourselves in Advanced Quilting and every quilt-making workshop within driving distance.

What started as a pleasant pastime became an all-consuming passion. Cutting, piecing, sewing, mixing and matching fabrics to see what creative wonder might appear took precedence over everything, including cooking.

This book began when the three of us sat, surrounded by our three-by-five cards, sharing recipes for quick and delicious dinners that would appease our families and prevent the uprising that was brewing from an overdose of fast foods.

While we don't have stainless-steel test kitchens, we have all tested each other's recipes and tried them on our severest critics—our husbands and children—who now are thinking maybe their wives and moms are gourmet chefs after all.

What they don't know is that some dinners are prepared early in the day, cook merrily along on their own while we quilt, and are ready to serve by dinnertime. Others of our meals require our undivided attention for about an hour or less just before serving. And you know what we do with the extra time.

Today's quilters have the advantage of many time savers. While we haven't mentioned them specifically in our recipes, we assume you would use blenders, food processors, any time saving-appliance or other gadget you may have plus willing children to help with the preparation.

Menus, like quilt making, may be changed as you go along. Size of appetites can require various quantities, and geography and seasons may warrant substitutions. Thumb through the menus until you find a dessert, for instance, that is compatible with what your market or your cupboard has to offer. Where we haven't included a recipe, use your own favorite.

We have served all these dinners and they worked for us—now all our beds have quilts. And they can work for you. Cook and quilt—enjoy them both.

Miriam Layton
Patricia A. Walker
Marion Williams

May 1982

The I'd-Rather-Be-Quilting Cookbook

French Star

The French Star might have been so named because it reminded someone of the medal on a French general's chest. In any case, there's no doubt of the origin of Coq au Vin in a French kitchen.

MENU
COQ AU VIN
ASPARAGUS WITH LEMON BUTTER
HOT ROLLS OR BISCUITS
POTS DE CRÈME

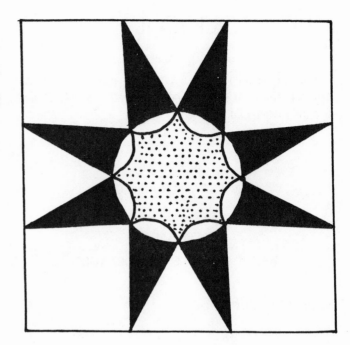

Coq au Vin

3 chicken breasts, split
1 teaspoon salt
3 tablespoons flour
1 cup sour cream
1 10¾-ounce can cream of mushroom soup
½ cup white wine or sherry
1 3-ounce can sliced mushrooms
  or ½ pound fresh mushrooms, sliced
Chopped parsley

Place chicken in baking dish. Mix all other ingredients except parsley and pour over chicken. Bake uncovered at 325° for 1 hour or until done. Garnish with the parsley. Serves 4-6.

Asparagus with Lemon Butter

1 pound fresh asparagus
6 tablespoons butter
Lemon juice

Wash and trim asparagus. Cook in boiling salted water until tender but still a little crisp, about 10 minutes. Drain and keep warm. Melt butter and add lemon juice to taste. Pour over asparagus and serve warm. Serves 4.

Pots de Crème

¾ cup milk
1 cup (6-ounce package) chocolate chips
1 egg
2 tablespoons sugar
1 teaspon vanilla
Pinch of salt

Heat milk to boiling. Place all other ingredients in blender and add the hot milk. Blend at low speed for 1 minute. Pour into 4 small cups or *pots de crème* (generally available wherever cooking supplies are sold). Chill thoroughly. Serve with a dash of whipped cream or a few chocolate sprinkles.

QUILTING HINT: *Do all your quilt pressing over a double thickness of turkish toweling. Tiny puckers will disappear.*

Trip Around the World

Trip Around the World gets its name from the different-hued squared "circles." Our menu goes around the world to China, France, Greece and Iraq.

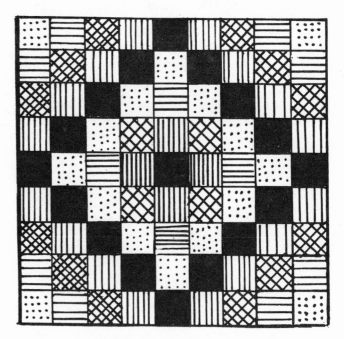

MENU

CHINESE MEATBALL SOUP

FRENCH BREAD

GREEK SALAD

BAGHDAD DATES WITH ORANGES

Chinese Meatball Soup

1 *pound ground beef*
1 *tablespoon cornstarch*
1 *egg*
3 *tablespoons soy sauce*
1 *small onion, minced*
2 *quarts beef broth, boiling*
½ *cup bean thread noodles*
2 *cups Chinese cabbage, roughly chopped*

Combine beef, cornstarch, egg, soy sauce and minced onion; mix well and form into meatballs. Drop meatballs into boiling beef broth. Boil gently, about 20 to 30 minutes, until meatballs rise to surface. Meanwhile, cover noodles with boiling water and soak until limp, 20 to 30 minutes. Drain and add to soup. Add cabbage to soup for 1 or 2 minutes — a short enough time to leave it crisp. Ladle into soup bowls. Serves 4.

Greek Salad

Add some crumbled feta cheese and Greek olives to assorted greens and top with your favorite oil and vinegar dressing to which some fresh or dried basil, oregano or marjoram has been added.

Baghdad Dates with Oranges

Pitted dates — 6 per person
Shelled walnut halves
Lemon juice
Powdered sugar
1 11-ounce can mandarin oranges, drained and chilled

Stuff each pitted date with half a walnut. Sprinkle with lemon juice and heat in oven at 350° until very hot, about 10 minutes. Dust with powdered sugar. Serve in small dessert dishes surrounded with chilled mandarin oranges or fresh orange slices.

QUILTING HINT: *Make a felt-covered board on which to arrange patches in trial combinations. The patches will stick to the felt and give you a chance to see how different fabrics work together.*

4

Fish Block

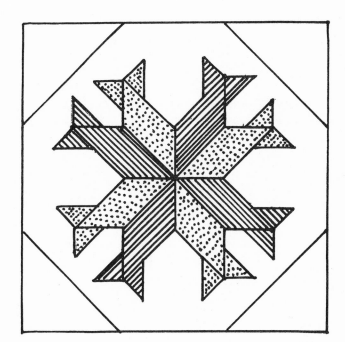

The Fish Block originated in New England, where fishing provided a living for many families. This menu will net you nothing but compliments.

MENU

FILLET OF SOLE VERONIQUE

BROILED TOMATOES WITH
DILL SOUR CREAM SAUCE

CUCUMBER AND GREENS SALAD

COFFEE TORTONI

Fillet of Sole Veronique

6 fillets of sole
2 tablespoons each chopped onion and butter
½ teaspoon salt
Dash of pepper
¾ cup dry white wine, divided
1 tablespoon butter
4 teaspoons flour
⅓ cup nonfat dry milk
1 cup seedless green grapes

Preheat oven to 350°. Butter bottom of 2-inch-deep casserole. Spread onion on bottom. Season fish with salt and pepper. Fold fillets in half, securing with toothpicks if necessary. Place on top of onions. Pour ½ cup wine over the fish. Cover with waxed paper cut to fit top of casserole and bake 20 minutes. Remove fish to warm platter. Stir butter, flour and dry milk into liquid left in casserole. When smooth, add ¼ cup wine and cook, stirring, until thickened. Return fish to sauce, arrange grapes around fillets and reheat under broiler until sauce bubbles, about 1 minute. Serves 6.

Broiled Tomatoes with Dill Sour Cream Sauce

½ cup sour cream
¼ cup mayonnaise
2 tablespoons finely chopped onion
¼ teaspoon dried dill weed
¼ teaspoon salt
3 large firm ripe tomatoes

Salt and pepper
Margarine or butter

Combine sour cream, mayonnaise, onion, dill and salt. Mix well and chill. Core tomatoes and cut in half crosswise. Season with salt, pepper and bits of margarine or butter. Broil 3 inches from heat for 5 minutes or until hot. Spoon sauce over tomatoes. Serves 6.

Coffee Tortoni

1 egg white
1 tablespoon instant coffee
⅛ teaspoon salt
2 tablespoons sugar
1 cup heavy cream
¼ cup sugar
1 teaspoon vanilla
⅛ teaspoon almond extract
¼ cup toasted almonds, finely chopped

Beat egg white, coffee and salt until stiff but not dry. Gradually add sugar and beat until satiny. In separate bowl, beat cream, sugar, vanilla and almond extract until stiff. Fold into egg-white mixture. Pour into 8 2-ounce paper cups. Sprinkle almonds on top of each cup. Freeze for one hour.

QUILTING HINT: When assembling patchwork pieces, press seams in one direction only. Pressing them open weakens the seam.

Dresden Plate

Dresden Plate gets its name from its shape. If fabric with small blue or pink flowers is used, it lends even more to the illusion. Bake the tart in a fluted pan and it might remind you of this pattern.

MENU

SPINACH AND RICOTTA CHEESE TART

CARROT SALAD

FRESH FRUIT

CHOCOLATE CRISPS

Spinach and Ricotta Cheese Tart

1 baked pie shell
2 10-ounce packages frozen chopped spinach
   or 3 bunches fresh spinach
¼ cup minced onion
3 tablespoons butter or margarine
¼ teaspoon salt
Dash of pepper
¼ teaspoon ground nutmeg
1 15-ounce container ricotta cheese
½ cup grated Parmesan cheese
1 cup half and half
3 eggs, slightly beaten
Snipped parsley
Cherry tomatoes, halved

Cook spinach according to package directions. Bounce up and down in a strainer to squeeze out all liquid. Sauté onions in butter until transparent. Stir in spinach, salt, pepper and nutmeg. In a bowl, combine cheeses, half and half and eggs. Stir in spinach and pour into baked pie shell. Bake 50 minutes at 350°, or until set and slightly browned. Garnish with parsley and cherry tomatoes wreathed around the tart. Serve hot or warm. Serves 6.

Carrot Salad

6 carrots, grated
½ cup coarsely chopped peanuts
½ cup seedless raisins
½ teaspoon salt
Dash of pepper
1 tablespoon lemon juice
Dressing
½ cup yogurt
½ cup sour cream

Mix together salad ingredients. Combine yogurt and sour cream and toss with salad. Serves 6.

Chocolate Crisps

1 12-ounce package semi-sweet chocolate morsels
⅓ cup crunchy peanut butter
6 cups cornflakes

Combine chocolate morsels and peanut butter and melt in a double boiler. Add to cornflakes, mix with a fork and drop by teaspoonfuls on waxed paper. Chill until firm.

QUILTING HINT: *Hold a pieced block up to a mirror for an objective look in selecting combinations of fabrics.*

Feathered Star

Feathered Star is a beautiful but difficult quilt block to piece. It has almost as many pieces as chickens have feathers. But Tarragon Chicken is easy as pie, and it's part of a beautiful meal plan.

MENU

TARRAGON CHICKEN

BUTTERED NOODLES

MANDARIN SALAD

HOT POPPY-SEED ROLLS

BAKED APPLES

Tarragon Chicken

6 chicken legs with thighs or 6 breast halves
Melted butter or salad oil
Juice of ½ lemon
¾ teaspoon dried tarragon or 2 teaspoons fresh
Salt and pepper

Brush chicken pieces generously with melted butter or oil. Sprinkle with lemon juice, tarragon, salt and pepper. Bake at 350° for 45 minutes. Serves 6.

Mandarin Salad

½ cup sliced almonds
1 tablespoon plus 1 teaspoon sugar
¼ head iceberg lettuce
¼ head romaine or butter lettuce
1 cup chopped celery
2 green onions and tops, thinly sliced
1 11-ounce can mandarin orange segments, drained
Dressing
¼ cup salad oil
2 tablespoons vinegar
2 tablespoons sugar
1 tablespoon snipped parsley
¼ teaspoon salt
Dash pepper
Dash hot pepper sauce

Cook almonds and sugar over low heat, stirring constantly until sugar is melted and almonds are coated. Put on waxed paper, cool, then break apart. Combine remaining ingredients in salad bowl. Combine dressing ingredients and shake well. Pour dressing over greens; toss to coat evenly. Top with sugared almonds and serve at once. Serves 6.

Baked Apples

6 tart apples
1 cup sugar
1 cup water
¼ cup currant or other tart jelly
1 tablespoon sherry (optional)
Finely chopped walnuts

Core apples and peel ⅔ of the way down. Combine sugar, water and jelly and boil for 5 minutes. Simmer apples in the syrup for 15 minutes. Put apples and syrup in a deep baking dish, cover and bake at 350° for 30 minutes, or until soft but not mushy. When cool, pour sherry over apples and sprinkle with nuts. Serves 6.

QUILTING HINT: To cut four or more patches at one time, iron and pin the fabric layers together. Pressing with a hot iron "welds" them briefly. Mark only the top layer of fabric and cut through the multiple layers with sharp scissors.

Lafayette Orange Peel

Lafayette Orange Peel has a romantic origin. At a formal ball, the Marquis de Lafayette presented his young dancing partner with an orange — a treasured token in those days. The quilt pattern was designed to commemorate the occasion. Sliced oranges frosted with shredded coconut make a memorable dessert.

MENU
BEEF-EGGPLANT CARMELO

BEAN SPROUT SALAD WITH WATERCRESS

CRUSTY ROLLS

FROSTED ORANGE SLICES

Beef-Eggplant Carmelo

1 pound ground beef
½ cup each chopped onion and celery
1 8-ounce can tomato sauce
½ cup water
¼ cup minced parsley
½ teaspoon each oregano and chili powder
1 eggplant, peeled and cut into ½-inch slices
4 ounces grated cheddar cheese

Brown beef, onion and celery. Drain off fat. Stir in tomato sauce, water, parsley and seasonings. Put meat mixture in a casserole. Sprinkle eggplant with salt and pepper and press down on top of meat mixture. Cover and bake at 350° for 20 minutes. Uncover and top with grated cheese. Return to oven until cheese melts. Serves 4.

Bean Sprout Salad

½ pound fresh bean sprouts
½ cup each sliced celery and chopped green onions
Chopped almonds
Paprika
1 bunch watercress

Dressing
¼ cup mayonnaise
1 teaspoon curry powder
2 tablespoons soy sauce
1 teaspoon powdered sugar
1 teaspoon lemon juice

Combine sprouts, celery and onions. (If canned bean sprouts are used, rinse with cold water and drain thoroughly.) Mix together dressing ingredients and toss with salad. Sprinkle with almonds and paprika and serve ringed with watercress. Serves 4.

Frosted Orange Slices

1 orange per person
Sherry or white wine
Grated coconut

Peel oranges, remove all white skin and cut into thin slices. Dribble sherry or wine over oranges. Top with grated coconut.

QUILTING HINT: When pressing patches, let the heat and steam do the work. Don't wiggle and move the iron about unnecessarily lest the unjoined edges get stretched.

Mexican Cross

The Mexican Cross probably was designed during Mexican War days: 1846 to 1848. Tacos are much older — but taco salad seems to be a fairly recent invention. It will win you lots of friends.

MENU
CONSOMMÉ OLÉ

TACO SALAD WITH AVOCADO DRESSING

TORTILLA CRACKER BREAD (page 33)

LEMON BARS

Consommé Olé

1 10½-ounce can beef broth
1 8-ounce bottle clam juice
4 tablespoons whipped cream

Combine beef broth and clam juice and heat until piping hot. Serve in small cups with a tablespoon of whipped cream floating on top. Serves 4.

Taco Salad

1 pound ground beef
¾ head iceberg lettuce, chopped
1 2¼-ounce can chopped or sliced black olives
3 green onions, minced
½ cup cheddar cheese, grated
2 cups chopped tomatoes
2 cups regular-size tortilla chips

Avocado Dressing

1 avocado, mashed
1 tablespoon lemon juice
½ cup sour cream
⅓ cup salad oil
2 shakes garlic powder
1 shake Tabasco sauce
½ teaspoon sugar
3 teaspoons chili powder
½ teaspoon salt

Fry beef until browned; drain on paper towel. Combine beef with all other salad ingredients except tortilla chips. Mix dressing until creamy, pour over salad and mix well. Top with tortilla chips and serve immediately. Serves 4.

Lemon Bars

¾ cup butter or margarine
½ cup powdered sugar
1½ cups flour
3 eggs, slightly beaten
1½ cups sugar
2 teaspoons flour
2 to 3 tablespoons lemon juice
Powdered sugar

Combine butter or margarine, ½ cup powdered sugar and 1½ cups flour; mix with fork until mixture resembles coarse cornmeal. Pat into a 9-by-12-inch ungreased pan. Bake 20 minutes at 350°. While it bakes, mix eggs, sugar, 2 teaspoons flour and lemon juice. Pour over hot crust and bake an additional 20 minutes. Sprinkle with powdered sugar while hot. Cut into squares or bars. Makes 24 bars.

QUILTING HINT: When tracing around templates with a pencil, instead of using the point of the lead, slide the pencil along on its side. The fabric will shift less as it is being marked.

Drunkard's Path

Drunkard's Path — *a complicated pattern made of many simple patches — has a lot of variations including Country Husband, Doves and Steppingstones. There are as many variations of Beef Burgundy. This one has the subtle flavor of great cuisine, but couldn't be simpler.*

MENU

BRANDIED BEEF BURGUNDY

RICE PILAF

FRESH VEGETABLE PLATE

APPLE CRUNCH

Brandied Beef Burgundy

3 pounds stewing beef, cut in 1-inch cubes
1 cup Burgundy
1 10¾-ounce can cream of mushroom soup
1 package onion soup mix
2 tablespoons brandy

Combine all ingredients in casserole. Cover and bake at 325° for 3½ hours or until tender. Serves 6-8.

Rice Pilaf

1 large onion, finely chopped
½ cup butter or margarine
1½ cups raw rice
¼ teaspoon each dried marjoram and rosemary, crumbled
1½ cups beef consommé
1½ cups water

Brown chopped onions lightly in butter. Add rice and seasonings; stir constantly until slightly browned, about 4 or 5 minutes. Add rest of ingredients, cover and bake at 325° for 45 minutes to 1 hour or until rice is done. Serves 6-8.

Apple Crunch

8 sliced apples (or 1 21-ounce can apple pie filling)
⅔ cup flour
1 teaspoon cinnamon
1 cup brown sugar
⅔ cup margarine
1 cup uncooked oats, reguar or quick
Cream or vanilla ice cream

Place sliced apples or apple pie filling in buttered 9-by-9-inch glass baking dish. Combine flour, cinnamon and sugar; cut in margarine until it resembles coarse oatmeal. Add oats and mix thoroughly. Spread over apples, pressing down firmly. Bake at 350° for 40 minutes for fresh apples, 25 minutes for apple pie filling. Top should be crisp and lightly browned. Serve warm topped with cream, whipped or plain, or vanilla ice cream. Serves 6.

QUILTING HINT: *When seaming dark and light fabrics together, always press both seam allowances away from the lighter fabric side so the dark fabric won't show through.*

Fruit Basket

Fruit Basket is an old favorite. It represents its name best when pieced in yellows, oranges and red. Curried Fruit complements perfectly these ham slices with spinach.

MENU
HAM SLICES IN CREAM AND WINE SAUCE

CURRIED FRUIT

HOT FRENCH BREAD

BROWNIES

Ham Slices in Cream and Wine Sauce

6 slices cooked ham, ¼ inch thick
3 tablespoons butter
2 packages frozen chopped spinach
3 tablespoons flour
1 tablespoon finely chopped green onions
1½ cups beef bouillon
½ cup dry red wine
⅛ teaspoon pepper
1 tablespoon ketchup
1 cup cream or half and half

Cook frozen spinach according to package directions and keep warm. Sauté ham slices lightly in butter. Set aside. Add flour and green onions to skillet and cook for 3 minutes. Warm bouillon and wine, add to flour mixture and heat until smooth, stirring constantly. Add pepper and ketchup, bring to simmer and slowly add cream or half and half. Simmer until sauce is slightly thickened. Add ham slices to reheat. Make a bed of cooked spinach on warmed serving platter, place ham slices on top and pour sauce over ham. Serves 6.

Curried Fruit

Prepare this a day in advance so flavors can blend.

1 8-ounce can pear halves
1 8-ounce can sliced peaches or apricots
1 8-ounce can pineapple chunks
10 maraschino cherries, halved
3 tablespoons margarine

1 tablespoon brown sugar
1 to 2 teaspoons curry powder

Drain fruit and reserve syrup. Place fruit in an ovenproof serving dish. Bring margarine, brown sugar, curry powder and 1 cup reserved syrup to a boil. Pour over fruit and heat, uncovered, at 325° until thoroughly hot, about 30 minutes. Just before serving, reheat at 350° for 20 minutes. Serves 6.

Brownies

1 cup sugar
½ cup butter
2 squares cooking chocolate
2 eggs
½ teaspoon salt
½ cup flour
1 teaspoon vanilla
1 cup walnuts, chopped

In heavy saucepan, melt sugar, butter and chocolate over low heat. Remove from heat and beat in eggs, salt, flour, vanilla and walnuts. Pour into greased 8-by-8-inch pan. Bake 20 minutes at 350° or 40 minutes at 325°. When cool, cut into squares.

COOKING HINT: Save syrup drained from canned fruits and use in gelatin salads, dessert sauces, or ices, or freeze into cubes for use in lemonade or punch.

Indian Hatchet

Indian Hatchet is a simple but extremely beautiful and effective pattern. It is easy to see how it got its name. Only an expert should hunt for mushrooms in the forest as the Indians did—mushrooms are most safely found in the produce department of the closest grocery.

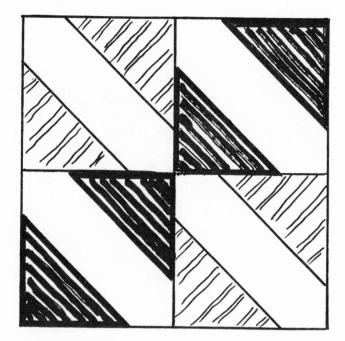

MENU

BEEF AND LIMA BEAN CASSEROLE

HERB-STUFFED MUSHROOMS

ORANGE SHERBET

VANILLA WAFERS

Beef and Lima Bean Casserole

1 package frozen baby lima beans
1½ teaspoons salt, divided
½ teaspoon pepper, divided
4 tablespoons margarine, divided
2 slices bread, white or wheat
¼ cup milk
1 egg
2 cloves garlic, minced
1 pound ground beef
1 cup sour cream
Parsley, chopped

Cook lima beans according to package directions. Drain, season with ½ teaspoon salt, ¼ teaspoon pepper and 3 tablespoons margarine. Soak bread in milk. In a bowl, beat the egg slightly, add remaining salt and pepper and garlic. Squeeze excess milk from bread; add bread to egg mixture along with ground beef. Mix and shape into walnut-sized balls, handling as lightly as possible. Melt remaining margarine in skillet and sauté meatballs until evenly browned. Transfer to a casserole and spoon lima beans on top. Bake, covered, at 350° for 30 minutes. Spread sour cream over beans and bake, uncovered, 5 minutes longer. Sprinkle with chopped parsley. Serves 4.

Herb-Stuffed Mushrooms

12 large fresh mushrooms
4 tablespoons margarine, divided
2 tablespoons finely chopped green onions
¾ cup fresh bread crumbs
⅓ cup chopped parsley
½ teaspoon sweet basil, dried
¼ teaspoon salt
Dash of pepper

Wipe mushrooms with a damp sponge. Remove stems and chop fine. Melt 2 tablespoons margarine in a skillet. Sauté mushroom tops briefly on both sides until they barely begin to color and are well coated with butter. Place in small baking dish. In the skillet, melt remaining margarine and briefly cook the mushroom stems and onions. Remove from heat, add bread crumbs, parsley, basil, salt and pepper and toss to mix. Spoon into mushroom caps and bake at 350° for 20 minutes. Serves 4.

COOKING HINT: *Sour cream with fewer calories? This has about a third as many as the real thing: to a pint of low-fat cottage cheese add ½ cup buttermilk and a pinch of salt. Whir in a blender until smooth—instant creamy ''sour cream.''*

Melon Patch

Melon Patch is another pattern whose design closely represents a familiar object. A few mint leaves picked from the moist end of the herb garden will make a honeydew melon perfect.

MENU
ORANGE CHICKEN

STEAMED RICE

BUTTERED SPINACH

MINTED MELON SLICES

Orange Chicken

1 frying chicken, quartered
1 green pepper, chopped
1 6-ounce can frozen orange juice, thawed
2 tablespoons cornstarch

Arrange chicken in a single layer in a baking dish. Sprinkle green pepper around chicken. Mix undiluted orange juice with cornstarch and pour over chicken. Cover and bake at 375° for 45 minutes. Baste with pan juices and serve. Serves 4.

Buttered Spinach

2 packages frozen leaf spinach
4 tablespoons butter
Salt and pepper
Nutmeg or grated lemon peel

Cook spinach according to package directions. Drain thoroughly. Melt butter in pot and add spinach, stirring to coat well. Salt and pepper to taste and add a touch of nutmeg or grated lemon peel. Serves 4.

Minted Melon Slices

1 honeydew melon, cut in wedges
2 tablespoons lemon juice
1 tablespoon fresh mint leaves, chopped

Arrange melon slices in shallow dish; sprinkle with lemon juice and chopped mint. Chill until ready to serve.

COOKING HINT: When possible, cook in decorative pots and pans, carrying them directly to the table. This saves on dishwashing and the food keeps warmer.

Rocky Road to Dublin

Rocky Road to Dublin is one of the dozens of patterns made by arranging the basic square used here in different ways; Robbing Peter to Pay Paul is probably the best known. Wind up this pork casserole meal with everyone's favorite—Rocky Road ice cream.

MENU

PARTY PORK CHOPS

CORN ON THE COB

TOMATOES WITH BASIL

ROCKY ROAD ICE CREAM

Party Pork Chops

4 lean, thick pork chops
Oil
1 cup raw rice
Salt and pepper
4 onion slices
Ketchup
⅛ teaspoon cayenne pepper
2 cups chicken stock

Brown chops in oil. Remove from pan and pour off all but 2 tablespoons fat. Add rice to pan and stir until lightly browned. Salt and pepper to taste. Transfer rice to ovenproof dish; put pork chops in single layer on top of rice. Place onion slice on each chop and a dash of ketchup on each onion slice. Sprinkle with cayenne pepper. Bring chicken stock to boil and pour around chops. Cover tightly and bake at 350° for 45 minutes or until all liquid is absorbed. Serves 4.

Tomatoes with Basil

3 firm, ripe tomatoes
1 tablespoon snipped fresh basil
Oil and vinegar

Slice tomatoes in ¼-inch slices, arrange on serving plate and sprinkle with basil. Drizzle lightly with oil and vinegar. Serves 4.

COOKING HINT: Rice should not be rinsed either before or after cooking because that washes away minerals and vitamins.

Tall Ships

Tall Ships is one of many patterns that represent a familiar object or scene. These pineapple boats are more like hollowed-out logs than ketches, but they're scrumptious, in any case.

MENU
OVEN STEW

BROWN BREAD

PINEAPPLE BOATS

Oven Stew

3-3½ pounds cubed beef

1 16-ounce can tomatoes

1 cup diced celery

5 carrots, cut in chunks

4 potatoes, peeled and cut in chunks

3 onions, chopped

½ cup beef broth

1 tablespoon salt

⅛ teaspoon each garlic powder, celery salt, pepper, dried oregano, dried thyme

¾ cup red wine

4 tablespoons quick-cooking tapioca

Put all ingredients into a large, ovenware pot. Cover and bake 5 hours at 250°. Serves 6.

Pineapple Boats

Cut top and bottom off one large, fresh pineapple. Cut in half lengthwise and divide each half in thirds lengthwise. Remove core. Cut fruit free about ½ inch from skin and leave in place. Slice fruit downward in wedges to retain boat shape. If pineapple needs sweetening, sprinkle with powdered sugar. Serve chilled.

COOKING HINT: *Fresh pineapple, salad greens, radishes, tomatoes, celery, cabbage and cucumbers do not freeze succussfully.*

Washington's Quilt

Washington's Quilt is one of the many designed to celebrate a presidential election. It is an easy design to put together— much like Gourmet Corned Beef, which has lots of ingredients but is simple to prepare. It would be great for a picnic on the Fourth of July, when we might be thinking of our first president.

MENU

CHILLED GOURMET CORNED BEEF

RELISH TRAY

GREEN BEANS VINAIGRETTE

BUTTERED SOFT ROLLS

FRESH CHERRIES

Gourmet Corned Beef

Prepare beef a day in advance.

3-4 pound corned beef brisket
¼ teaspoon oregano
¼ teaspoon rosemary
¼ teaspoon dill seed
1 bay leaf
6 whole cloves
1 stick cinnamon
2 cloves garlic
1 medium onion, quartered
2 stalks celery, cut in half
½ orange, unpeeled

Put all ingredients in a large pot, cover with water and simmer 3 to 4 hours. Let beef cool in liquid, remove, wrap in foil and refrigerate. Slice thinly on the bias and serve cold. Serves 4-6.

Relish Tray

On a tray, arrange several of the following: ripe olives, sweet or sour pickles, green olives, radishes, cherry tomatoes, celery, cheese cubes.

Green Beans Vinaigrette

2 packages frozen string beans, julienne
½ cup French dressing
1 tablespoon minced fresh parsley or chives

Cook beans according to directions on the package. Drain well. Mix dressing with herbs and pour over beans. Cover and store in refrigerator overnight. Serves 4-6.

COOKING HINT: *Eliminate mincing or slicing garlic by running the cloves through with toothpicks before adding them to other ingredients, then discard them after cooking.*

Burgoyne Surrounded

Burgoyne Surrounded was designed to celebrate the Battle of Saratoga and victory in the American Revolution for the Red, White and Blue—the usual colors used in this quilt. Celebrate again with a red, white and blue parfait.

MENU
CHICKEN SCALOPPINE

BUTTERED NOODLES

HERBED CUCUMBER SALAD

RED, WHITE AND BLUE PARFAITS

Chicken Scaloppine

2 whole chicken breasts, halved and boned
Salt and pepper
4 tablespoons butter
1 cup heavy cream
⅓ cup sherry
¼ pound mushrooms, sliced

Skin chicken breasts and pound until slightly flattened. Season with salt and pepper. Heat butter to sizzling and sauté chicken 2 to 3 minutes on each side or until juices run clear. Remove to heated platter and keep warm. Sauté mushrooms in remaining butter until golden. Stir in cream and sherry and cook until slightly thickened. Pour sauce over chicken and serve with buttered noodles. Serves 4.

Herbed Cucumber Salad

3 cucumbers
3 tablespoons olive oil
3 tablespoons lemon juice
1 tablespoon fresh thyme or ½ teaspoon dried
¼ teaspoon pepper
½ teaspoon salt

Peel cucumbers and slice very thin. Pat dry with paper towels. Mix remaining ingredients and pour over cucumbers. Chill. Serve in a bowl or on individual lettuce leaves. Serves 6.

Red, White and Blue Parfaits

1 pint strawberry ice cream
1 pint vanilla ice cream
1 pint blueberries

In individual parfait glasses, place a scoop of strawberry ice cream, then a scoop of vanilla and top with blueberries. Serves 4.

COOKING HINT: Pat dry any meat to be sautéed. Water will cause spattering.

Squire Smith's Choice

Squire Smith's Choice would certainly be these meat balls and noodles. It would be interesting to know who Squire Smith was and why he chose this pattern—we'd like to think it was because of the smile of whoever made the quilt.

MENU

SQUIRE SMITH'S MEAT BALLS

POPPY-SEED NOODLES

GREEN BEANS

APPLE COLE SLAW

RHUBARB CRISP

Squire Smith's Meat Balls

1 pound bottom round, ground
1 cup soft bread crumbs
½ cup milk
1 onion, minced
¼ cup cooking oil
½ teaspoon salt
⅛ teaspoon pepper
¼ cup Worcestershire sauce
1 cup ketchup
¼ cup sugar
2 tablespoons red wine or vinegar

Combine meat, bread crumbs, milk and minced onion. Mix thoroughly and form into 10 to 12 meatballs. Brown evenly in oil. Combine remaining ingredients and pour over meatballs. Cover and cook 10 minutes. Serves 4-6.

Poppy-Seed Noodles

6 to 8 ounces noodles
3 tablespoons butter
1 tablespoon poppy seeds

Follow package directions for cooking noodles. Drain well. Add butter and poppy seeds and toss. Serve piping hot. Serves 4-6.

Apple Cole Slaw

1 11-ounce can mandarin oranges
3 cups shredded cabbage
1 cup chopped apple
French dressing or mayonnaise

Thoroughly drain oranges. Mix cabbage, apple and oranges with dressing or mayonnaise. Chill well. Serves 4-6.

Rhubarb Crisp

2 cups rhubarb, cut in small pieces
2 tablespoons flour
¼ cup uncooked oats
¼ cup butter
¾ cup white sugar

Spread rhubarb over bottom of a small, greased pan. Combine remaining ingredients and mix until crumbly. Sprinkle over rhubarb and bake at 325° for about 40 minutes. Serve warm with cream or ice cream. Serves 4-6.

COOKING HINT: Blend a little lemon juice with mayonnaise or salad dressing—this combination, when warmed, makes an acceptable mock Hollandaise.

End of Day

End of Day represents the last rays of the sun and approaching night. We can enjoy our meal as the sun slowly sets and we reflect on another pleasant quilting day.

MENU
SUNSET SPAGHETTI

GARLIC BREAD

HEARTS OF LETTUCE WITH BLUE CHEESE DRESSING

MINIATURE CANDY BARS

Sunset Spaghetti

1 *pound hamburger*
2 *onions, chopped*
2 *tablespoons parsley*
2 *cloves garlic, crushed*
2 *8-ounce cans tomato sauce and 1 can water*
2 *6-ounce cans tomato paste*
1 *tablespoon Worcestershire sauce*
Salt and pepper
6 *to 8 ounces spaghetti or vermicelli*
Grated Parmesan cheese

Brown hamburger in 2 tablespoons cooking oil, add onions, parsley and garlic and simmer for 5 minutes. Add remaining ingredients, except spaghetti and cheese, and simmer 1 hour, covered. Cook spaghetti or vermicelli according to package directions. Have plenty of grated Parmesan cheese for topping. Serves 4.

Garlic Bread

Slice a loaf of French bread almost to the bottom crust. Spread both sides of slices generously with soft butter and sprinkle with Garlic Bread Sprinkle. Wrap in foil and heat in a 400° oven for 20 mintues or until heated through.

Hearts of Lettuce with Blue Cheese Dressing

1 *head iceberg lettuce*
2 *tablespoons mayonnaise*
2 *tablespoons blue cheese, crumbled*
¾ *cup oil-and-vinegar dressing*

Remove outer leaves of lettuce if bruised. Cut into wedges. Combine mayonnaise and blue cheese and add to oil and vinegar dressing. Pour over lettuce. Serves 4.

COOKING HINT: *When cooking macaroni or spaghetti, add a little oil to the water to prevent it from boiling over.*

Old Homestead

Old Homestead is an old-fashioned, sentimental pattern. This menu, from sausage to custard, is just as old-fashioned, comfortable—and good.

MENU
SAUSAGE AND APPLES

BAKED POTATOES

HARVARD BEETS

BAKED CUSTARD

Sausage and Apples

½ pound link sausages
3 apples, cored
⅓ cup white sugar
Cinnamon

Cover sausages with cold water in frying pan. Bring to a boil and drain. (This removes some of the grease.) Slice apples into a baking pan. Cover with sugar and sprinkle with cinnamon. Lay sausages on top of apples. Bake at 350° for 30 minutes or until apples are soft. Turn sausages once during baking. Serves 4.

Baked Potatoes

Scrub 4 medium potatoes with vegetable brush. Rub skins with butter or cooking oil if desired. Bake at 350° for 1½ hours. To serve, cut an X in top of each potato and insert a pat of butter.

Harvard Beets

½ cup sugar
1 tablespoon cornstarch
¼ cup mild vinegar or white wine
¼ cup water
10 small cooked beets, fresh or canned
2 tablespoons butter

In a saucepan, combine sugar and cornstarch. Add vinegar or wine and water; boil and stir until mixture thickens, about 5 mintues. Add beets and butter. Reheat until butter melts and beets are hot. Serves 4.

Baked Custard

2 eggs
3 tablespoons sugar
Dash salt
¼ teaspoon vanilla
2 cups milk
Nutmeg

Beat eggs slightly; add sugar, salt and vanilla. Heat milk and add to egg mixture. Pour into custard cups and sprinkle with nutmeg. Place cups in a shallow pan and pour in hot water to reach halfway up the sides of the cups. Bake at 350° for 40 minutes or until a silver knife inserted into the center of the custard comes out clean. Custards will thicken as they cool. Serves 4.

COOKING HINT: Whether your oven is heated by electricity, gas or wood, you'll save energy by filling up the oven every time you use it. It's easy to plan a menu with main dish, vegetable, and dessert all oven-cooked.

Pineapple

The Pineapple is an old symbol of hospitality, used in Colonial times for holiday table centerpieces. As a quilt pattern, it drew friends together. In this meal, it can be your symbol of friendship—and mouthwatering at the same time.

MENU
BAKED HAM STEAK

SCALLOPED PINEAPPLE

BUTTERED SWISS CHARD OR BEET GREENS

LEMON CUSTARD CUPS

Baked Ham Steak

1 ham steak, 1 inch thick
1 tablespoon brown sugar
1 cup cider, orange juice or juice from canned fruit

Spread sugar over top of ham. Bake in 375° oven for 1 hour, basting frequently with cider or fruit juice. Serves 4.

Scalloped Pineapple

1 8-ounce can crushed pineapple
¼ cup orange juice
½ cup brown sugar
4 slices bread torn into small pieces
  (reserve ⅓ cup for topping)
3 tablespoons melted butter, divided

Mix undrained pineapple with orange juice and brown sugar. Stir in bread pieces. Pour half the melted butter into a small baking dish. Add half the pineapple mixture; sprinkle with the remaining butter and another layer of pineapple. Top with reserved bread. Bake at 350° for 30 minutes or until thickened and lightly browned. Serves 4.

Buttered Swiss Chard or Beet Greens

Wash thoroughly one bunch Swiss chard or beet greens. If using chard, split coarse white center rib of each leaf lenghwise. Cook, covered, for about 15 minutes in enough water to keep it from burning (slightly more than what clings to leaves). Serve with melted butter and a dash of lemon juice. Serves 4.

Lemon Custard Cups

1 tablespoon melted butter
2 eggs, separated
3 tablespoons lemon juice
1 teaspoon grated lemon rind
⅛ teaspoon salt
½ cup sugar
3 tablespoons flour
1 cup milk

Combine butter, egg yolks and lemon juice. Mix well lemon rind, salt, sugar and flour. Add to butter-egg yolk mixture and stir in milk to blend. Beat egg whites until stiff but not dry. Fold into egg yolk mixture and turn into 4 buttered custard cups. Set in a pan of hot water and bake at 350° for 30 minutes. Chill in refrigerator. Serves 4.

COOKING HINT: Heat lemons before extracting juice for twice as much juice. Submerge lemons in boiling water or, if the oven is on, heat them briefly in the oven.

Ocean Waves

Ocean Waves is a simple pattern of repeated triangles of contrasting fabrics—an easy design, but one with a look of complexity. These scallops, also from the sea, are even simpler to prepare and ostentatiously smart, as were the Ritz hotels.

MENU
SCALLOPS À LA RITZ

CREAMED SPINACH

BAKED TOMATOES

CHERRY COBBLER

Scallops à la Ritz

1 pound scallops
1 cup Ritz cracker crumbs
1 stick melted butter

If scallops are large, cut in quarters. Roll in melted butter and then in cracker crumbs. Put in an oven-proof dish and bake at 350° for 10 minutes. Serves 4-6.

Creamed Spinach

2 packages frozen chopped spinach
4 ounces cream cheese
Grated nutmeg

Cook spinach according to package directions. Bounce up and down in a sieve to drain thoroughly. Return to pot and add cream cheese, cut into cubes. Toss together over low heat until cheese melts and blends with spinach. Add a light sprinkle of grated nutmeg. Serves 4-6.

Baked Tomatoes

4 ripe tomatoes, cut crosswise
2 tablespoons brown sugar
Salt and pepper
Dash of sweet basil, dried
Bread crumbs
1 tablespoon butter

Cut tomatoes in half. Put in greased baking dish or muffin tins. Sprinkle with brown sugar, salt, pepper, basil and bread crumbs. Put a little butter on each tomato. Bake at 350° for 20 minutes. Serves 4.

Cherry Cobbler

1 21-ounce can cherry pie filling
1 tablespoon fresh lemon juice
1 cup flour
½ cup chopped pecans or walnuts
⅓ cup butter or margarine
¼ cup firmly packed brown sugar
¾ teaspoon cinnamon
¼ teaspoon allspice
Vanilla ice cream

Combine pie filling and lemon juice in a shallow one-quart baking dish. Mix remaining ingredients except ice cream and sprinkle over pie filling. Bake at 350° until top is brown and cherries are bubbly, about 25 minutes. Serve warm topped with ice cream. Serves 4-6.

COOKING HINT: If you are out of brown sugar, just substitute white sugar with molasses added (two tablespoons molasses to ½ cup sugar).

Castle Wall

Castle Wall, carefully planned with alternating light and dark patches, will have a three-dimensional effect, much like turrets in a medieval castle. The lord is in his castle, home from a trip to India, introducing his family to lamb curry.

MENU
LAMB CURRY

RICE

CRISP GREEN SALAD

COLD LEMON SOUFFLÉ

Prepare curry and soufflé a day ahead.

Lamb Curry

2 pounds boneless lean lamb
3 tablespoons oil
1½ cups each chopped onion and celery
1 clove garlic, minced
1 cup chopped parsley
2 thick lemon slices
2 cups stock or chicken broth
1 teaspoon Worcestershire sauce
1 teaspoon tomato paste
¼ teaspoon thyme
1 tablespoon curry powder
 (or more, depending on your taste)
1 cup canned coconut milk

Brown lamb lightly in oil. Add onions, celery and garlic. Cook for 2 or 3 minutes. Add rest of the ingredients and cook, covered, over low heat, stirring occasionally, for 1½ hours or until lamb is tender. Reheat in top of a double boiler or over very low heat. Serve with several of the following condiments: grated coconut, chopped peanuts, chopped onion, chutney, sour cream, chopped bananas, raisins, chopped hard-boiled eggs, crumbled bacon. Serves 6.

Cold Lemon Soufflé

1 envelope unflavored gelatin
⅔ cup sugar, divided
¼ teaspoon salt
4 eggs, separated
½ cup lemon juice
¼ cup water
1 tablespoon grated lemond rind

In top of double boiler, mix gelatin, ⅓ cup sugar and salt. Beat egg yolks slightly; add lemon juice and water. Add to gelatin mixture and cook over boiling water, stirring, until mixture thickens, about 5 minutes. Remove from heat, add lemon rind and chill until mixture mounds slightly when dropped from a spoon. Beat egg whites until stiff. Gradually add remaining ⅓ cup sugar and beat until very stiff. Fold into chilled gelatin mixture. Put into serving dish and chill until firm. Serves 6.

COOKING HINT: Keep leftover cooked rice to add to green salads; with celery, green peppers and a bit of ham, if there is some, this makes a hearty dish.

Birds in Flight

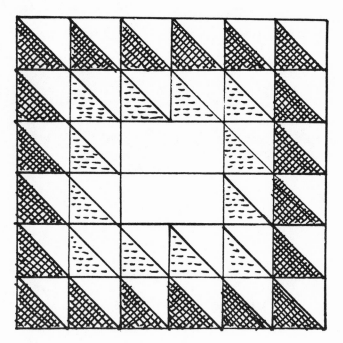

Birds in Flight took no imagination to name; it is easy to see the geese going north. But the bird from which this hot chicken salad is made never flew.

MENU

HOT CHICKEN SALAD

BREAD STICKS

PICKLED BEETS WITH ONION RINGS

FRESH FRUIT COMPOTE

Hot Chicken Salad

2 cups diced cooked chicken
¾ cup chopped walnuts
¾ cup chopped celery
3 teaspoons minced onion
3 tablespoons lemon juice
¾ cup mayonnaise
Salt and pepper to taste

Combine all ingredients and mix well. Put in individual casseroles or shells, top with dry bread crumbs and bake at 425° until lightly browned, about 15 minutes. Serves 4.

Pickled Beets with Onion Rings

1 can pickled beets
1 medium onion, thinly sliced

Drain beets. Separate onion slices into rings. Combine and serve on lettuce leaves. Serves 4.

Fresh Fruit Compote

Combine several fresh fruits—whatever the season offers. Sprinkle lightly with sugar and fresh lemon juice. Add a splash of sherry or wine.

COOKING HINT: A three-and-a-half-pound chicken will yield about 3 cups cooked chicken. Two chicken breasts, about 10 ounces each, will yield 1½ to 2 cups cooked chicken.

Delectable Mountains

The Delectable Mountains were a goal for the characters in John Bunyan's Pilgrim's Progress, and the name is appropriate for this delightful pattern. Though its origin is far from the mountains, this Seafood Bisque is delectable.

MENU
SEAFOOD BISQUE

BAGUETTES

SPINACH SALAD

MAPLE SUNDAES

Seafood Bisque

1 can condensed green pea soup
1 can condensed tomato soup
1 cup milk
1 cup half and half
½ cup dry sherry
1 cup flaked crabmeat or shrimp
Lemon slices

Combine soups; gradually stir in milk and half and half. Cook over low heat, stirring occasionally until soup bubbles. Stir in sherry and crab or shrimp. Reheat gently—do not let boil. Ladle into warmed soup bowls and top each with a thin slice of lemon. Serves 4.

Spinach Salad

1 bunch spinach
2 or 3 green onions, sliced thin
6 sliced fresh mushrooms
French dressing

Wash spinach thoroughly, pat dry and tear into bite-sized pieces. Combine with green onions and mushrooms; toss with your favorite French dressing. Serves 4.

Maple Sundaes

1 pint vanilla ice cream
Maple syrup
Whipped cream or non-dairy topping
Chopped nuts

For each serving, put a scoop of vanilla ice cream in a dish, pour over maple syrup and top with whipped cream or non-dairy topping. Sprinkle with chopped nuts. Serves 4.

COOKING HINT: *Combine two kinds of canned soup, as here, for new flavors. Good combinations are clam broth and cream of chicken or celery and cheddar cheese. Or spark up canned soup with grated nutmeg, curry, chili powder or sherry. Top at the last minute with crisp croutons, popcorn, chopped green onion, paprika or chives.*

Grandmother's Own

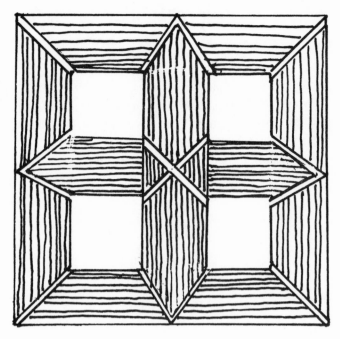

This pattern is Grandmother's Own. There's also Grandma's Tulip, Grandma's Red and White, Grandmother's Engagement Ring, Grandmother's Flower Garden—and lots more—handed down from one generation to the next. Mama Mia Casserole is like that.

MENU
ANTIPASTO

MAMA MIA CASSEROLE

HOT ITALIAN BREAD

SHERBET OR SPUMONI ICE CREAM

Antipasto

On a large plate, decoratively arrange at least 6 of the following: marinated artichoke hearts, radishes, sliced Italian salami, cherry tomatoes, black olives, pepperoncini, jack cheese strips, pickled beets, celery hearts, fresh mushrooms.

Mama Mia Casserole

1 *pound ground lean beef*
1 *tablespoon oil*
1 *large chopped onion*
1 *cup chopped celery with leaves*
¾ *cup grated carrots*
1 *2-pound can tomatoes*
1 *tablespoon salt*
¾ *teaspoon oregano*
½ *teaspoon pepper*
2 *cloves minced garlic*
1 *package frozen chopped spinach, partially thawed*
½ *cup grated Parmesan cheese*
¾ *pound noodles*

Brown beef in oil. Add chopped onions, celery and grated carrots. Cook 5 minutes. Stir in tomatoes, salt, oregano, pepper and garlic. Bring to a boil. Cover and simmer 30 minutes. While this cooks, prepare noodles according to the package directions; drain and set aside. Stir noodles and spinach into the cooked sauce, mix thoroughly. Put into a 2-by-9-by-13-inch baking dish, sprinkle cheese on top and bake at 350° for 30 minutes or until bubbly. Serves 8.

COOKING HINT: *Crush garlic between two layers of waxed paper and mash it with the broad side of a knife. That way there's no implement to clean.*

Lancaster Rose

To be authentic, the Lancaster Rose should be red, since Lancaster was symbolized by the red rose. Today the neighboring towns of Lancaster and York, Pennsylvania, playfully continue the Wars of the Roses. Our meal includes Mennonite Cabbage Salad, a favorite in the Pennsylvania Dutch country.

MENU
DELUXE HAMBURGERS
SESAME-SEED BUNS
MENNONITE CABBAGE SALAD
CHOCOLATE NUT SUNDAES

Deluxe Hamburgers

1 pound ground beef
½ cup sour cream
1 tablespoon chopped chives
Salt and pepper to taste

Mix all ingredients together and form into 4 patties. Fry hamburgers in a hot skillet. Serve on toasted sesame-seed buns wtih your favorite trimmings. Serves 4.

Mennonite Cabbage Salad

Make this the day before you plan to serve it.

1 small cabbage, shredded
1 small onion, chopped
1 green pepper, chopped
Celery seed
Salt and pepper
½ cup salad oil
½ cup vinegar
1 cup sugar

Arrange a layer of cabbage, onion and peppers in a bowl and season with celery seed, salt and pepper. Repeat layers and seasonings. Combine oil, vinegar and sugar and bring to a boil. Pour hot syrup over the cabbage mixture, cover, and let stand overnight in the refrigerator. Do not stir until the next morning. Keeps well for several days in the refrigerator. Makes 6-8 servings.

Chocolate Sauce (quick and easy)

½ cup cream or evaporated milk
½ cup light corn syrup
2 tablespoons butter or margarine
6 ounces semi-sweet chocolate morsels
Pinch of salt
1 teaspoon vanilla or peppermint flavoring

In a saucepan, combine cream, corn syrup and margarine and cook to a boil. Remove from heat; stir in chocolate morsels, salt and flavoring until chocolate is melted. Serve hot or cold over vanilla ice cream. Makes 1¼ cups sauce.

COOKING HINT: The dark outer leaves of cabbage, lettuce and other leafy vegetables are richest in minerals. Use them in soups if they're too unsightly for raw serving.

Clam Shell

The Clam Shell is used both as a pattern for a pieced block and as a design to quilt; the curved lines make it no easy block to piece. Cheater's Chowder is quick and easy and just as good as the old favorite, clam chowder.

MENU

CHEATER'S CHOWDER

PILOT CRACKERS

GREEN SALAD WITH TOMATO WEDGES

BANANAS CRANBERRY

Cheater's Chowder

2 slices bacon, diced
1 medium onion, chopped
1 10¾-ounce can cream of potato soup
1 soup can milk
1 6½-ounce can minced clams, drained
⅛ teaspoon pepper

Fry bacon and onion together until the onion is golden and the bacon lightly browned. Drain. Add one can of milk to cream of potato soup and heat slowly. Add clams, bacon and onions, pepper; simmer 10 minutes, stirring occasionally. Ladle into warm bowls. Serves 2.

Pilot Crackers

Butter and toast crackers in oven. Serve hot.

Bananas Cranberry

½ can jellied cranberry sauce
2 peeled bananas

Put cranberry sauce through a sieve. Add ¾ cup water and boil sauce until slightly thickened, about 5 minutes. Slice bananas lengthwise and spoon cranberry sauce over them. Bake at 375° for 15 minutes and serve warm. Serves 2.

COOKING HINT: Store cereals and crackers in covered jars in a cupboard above the stove, if possible. The heat keeps them crisp.

Road to Oklahoma

The Road to Oklahoma may have first been put together by the wife of a Sooner on the way to open that state. It's also called New Four-Patch. Oklahoma Pot Roast makes a hearty meal for Sooners, Boomers or just plain growing people.

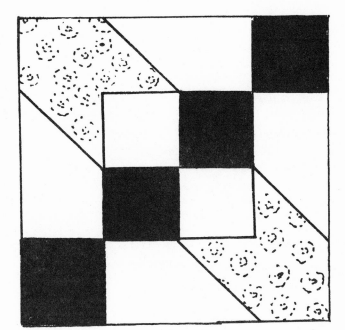

MENU

OKLAHOMA POT ROAST

BOILED POTATOES

BUTTERED MINTED CARROTS

BISCUITS

APPLESAUCE AND COOKIES

Oklahoma Pot Roast

4-5-pound roast
1 tablespoon cornstarch
1 tablespoon Worcestershire sauce
1 envelope onion soup mix
1 4-ounce can tomato sauce
½ can water
1 large onion, chopped
1 green pepper, chopped
1 clove garlic, minced

In a roasting pan, place roast on 2 layers of foil large enough to wrap roast completely. Mix together remaining ingredients and pour over meat. Seal foil, cover roasting pan, and bake 3 hours at 350°. Serves 6.

Buttered Minted Carrots

1 pound carrots
2 tablespoons butter
1 teaspoon lemon juice
2 teaspoons finely chopped fresh mint leaves
    or 1 teaspoon dried mint

Cook sliced carrots in boiling water until barely tender, about 20 minutes. Drain and add butter, lemon juice and mint leaves. Stir lightly and serve warm. Serves 6.

COOKING HINT: *Vegetables cut into small pieces will cook faster.*

World without End

World without End *is a phrase from the* Book of Common Prayer *("As it was in the beginning, is now, and ever shall be: World without end"). It's a simple block of alternating lights and darks that repeat throughout the quilt. The muffin batter here goes on and on and on—nearly without end.*

MENU
DOUBLE CONSOMMÉ WITH SHERRY

SEASONAL FRESH FRUIT SALAD

HONEY DRESSING

BRAN MUFFINS

CHEESECAKE

Double Consommé with Sherry

4 cans consommé, undiluted
Sherry

Simmer consommé 10 minutes until slightly reduced. Into each soup cup or mug, measure 1 tablespoon dry sherry and fill with very hot consommé. Stir and serve immediately. Serves 6.

Seasonal Fresh Fruit Salad

Slice several chilled fruits, such as pears, peaches, pineapple, bananas, melons or grapes, and arrange on a bed of lettuce. Prepare at the last minute so fruit looks fresh.

Honey Dressing

½ cup honey
½ cup mayonnaise
4 teaspoons dry mustard
¼ cup vinegar
¼ cup salad oil

Mix honey with mayonnaise. Mix mustard with vinegar and add oil. Combine the two mixtures, blending until smooth, and pour over fruit salad.

Bran Muffins

This batter will keep for a month or more in the refrigerator and makes dozens of muffins.

1 cup boiling water
3 cups All-Bran, divided
½ cup raisins
1 cup sugar
¼ cup honey
½ cup plus 1½ tablespoons margarine
2 eggs
2 cups buttermilk
3 cups flour
2½ teaspoons baking soda
1 teaspoon salt

Pour water over 1 cup All-Bran, add raisins, stir and set aside. In a large bowl, cream sugar, honey and margarine. Add eggs and beat well. Stir in buttermilk. Add bran/raisin mixture. Add flour, soda and salt sifted together. Add 2 cups bran and mix well. Cover tightly and store in refrigerator. To bake muffins: spoon into greased muffin tins or paper muffin cups, *without stirring batter.* Bake at 400° for 16 to 20 minutes.

COOKING HINT: *Eggs used in most recipes are assumed to be large, weighing two ounces.*

Rose of Sharon

"I am the rose of Sharon, and the lily of the valleys," says the Song of Solomon. The quilt given this name was a special one, part of many a bride's dower chest; she would use it only for company. This special meal deserves to be shared with company.

MENU
BAKED FISH FILLETS WITH ALMONDS

FROZEN SPINACH SOUFFLÉ

ONION AND BEET SALAD

FRESH OR FROZEN PEACHES

Baked Fish Fillets with Almonds

1 pound fish fillets, fresh or frozen
4 tablespoons butter, divided
2 tablespoons cornstarch
¼ teaspoon salt
Dash of cayenne pepper
1 cup milk
½ cup mild cheese, grated
1 tablespoon sherry
½ cup slivered almonds

Place fish fillets in shallow ovenproof dish. Make cream sauce (melt 2 tablespoons butter, add cornstarch, salt and cayenne, stir until smooth, add milk, stir until thickened and smooth, add cheese and wine, stir until cheese melts). Pour over fish fillets and bake at 375° for 20 minutes. Brown almonds in small skillet in 2 tablespoons butter. Just before serving, sprinkle almonds over fish. Serves 3.

Onion and Beet Salad

1 can sliced beets
1 medium onion
Salad greens
Oil and lemon dressing

Drain beets; slice onion very thin. Arrange on a bed of salad greens. Sprinkle with dressing.

Oil and Lemon Dressing

1 teaspoon salt
½ teaspoon pepper
½ teaspoon sugar
½ teaspoon dry mustard
1 clove garlic, minced
1 tablespoon lemon juice
½ cup salad oil

Mix all ingredients in a bottle and shake well to blend. Makes about ½ cup.

Peaches

Peaches may be flavored with ⅓ cup Marsala wine and sprinkled with sugar to taste.

COOKING HINT: When buying filleted fish, allow one-third pound per serving.

World's Fair

World's Fair won first prize at the Chicago world's fair in 1893. The pattern should more properly be called World's Columbian Exposition, to distinguish it from many other fair prize-winners. If the apple pie here were ever entered in competition in a world's fair, it would be a sure winner, too.

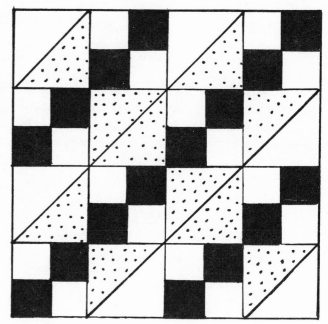

MENU
SHRIMP COCKTAIL

TURKEY SUPRÊME

RICE PILAF

BUTTERED CARROTS

CRUMB-TOP APPLE PIE

Shrimp Cocktail

1 pound small shelled shrimp, cooked
1 green onion, minced
1 tablespoon chopped parsley
¾ cup ketchup
1 tablespoon prepared horseradish
1 tablespoon lemon juice

Mix shrimp with onion and parsley and spoon into stemmed glasses. Combine ketchup, horseradish and lemon juice and pour over shrimp. Chill until serving. Serves 6.

Turkey Suprême

2 packages frozen broccoli, thawed
6 or more thin slices of turkey white meat
¼ cup butter
¼ cup flour
2 cups milk, warmed
¼ cup dry sherry
2 cups sharp cheese, grated

Arrange broccoli in the bottom of six individual ovenware serving dishes or one large baking dish. Place turkey slices on top of broccoli. Melt butter and stir in flour. Remove from heat and add milk,

stirring until smooth. Return to heat and continue cooking over medium heat until mixture thickens, stirring constantly; add sherry. Pour sauce over turkey and sprinkle cheese over the top. Bake at 350° for 15 minutes or until heated through and cheese is lightly browned. Serves 6.

Crumb-Top Apple Pie

6 tart apples, peeled and sliced thin
1 unbaked pie shell
½ cup sugar
½ cup graham cracker crumbs
¼ cup flour
¼ cup walnut meats, chopped
Pinch salt
½ stick melted butter

Place apple slices in pie shell. Mix together all ingredients except butter. Spoon and pat over apples. Pour melted butter over all and bake at 350° for 45 minutes to an hour. Serve warm or cool. Serves 6.

COOKING HINT: Cooking oil mixed half and half with butter or margarine for sautéing prevents the butter from burning. Use this combination for browning rice for pilafs.

Milky Way

Milky Way is a reminder of the stars in the sky on a cloudless night: the finished quilt is a whirl of pinwheels. An ice-cream bar is the milky way to end this spicy meal.

MENU

ENCHILADA CASSEROLE

TORTILLA CRACKER BREAD

BUTTER LETTUCE SALAD

Enchilada Casserole

1 10-ounce can Mexican style tomato sauce
  or enchilada sauce
1 can water
1 8-ounce can tomato sauce
1 pound ground beef
1 large onion, chopped
2 garlic cloves, chopped
1 hard-cooked egg, chopped
1 4½-ounce can chopped ripe olives
½ teaspoon salt
12 corn tortillas
½ pound Monterey jack or cheddar cheese, grated

Heat tomato sauces and water. Brown meat, onion and garlic together. Add egg, olives, salt and ½ cup sauce to meat. Dip whole tortillas in remaining sauce; in a 2-quart casserole, put a layer of tortillas, meat and cheese, reserving ½ cup cheese for top. Repeat layers two more times. Pour remaining sauce over and cover with reserved cheese. Bake at 350° for 25 minutes. Serves 4-6.

Tortilla Cracker Bread

8 to 12 flour tortillas

Set oven rack in top position. Heat oven to 350°. Spread tortillas in a single layer on rack. Bake 4 to 5 minutes or until crisp. Serve hot.

COOKING HINT: When hard-boiling eggs, avoid hard, rubbery whites by putting the eggs into cold water to cover, then bringing them to a simmer for 20 minutes. Don't let the water boil. Plunge eggs into cold running water and leave them in the cold water until cool before peeling.

Next-door Neighbor

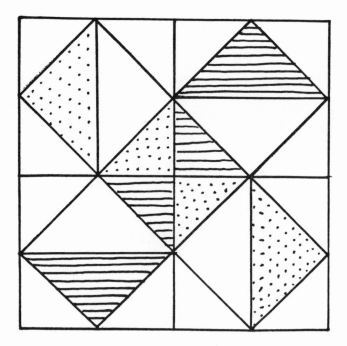

Next-door Neighbor is a simple pattern requiring effective use of contrasting fabrics to make it an outstanding quilt. The name suggests that it was a pattern borrowed from the woman next door. Like most recipes, this fish dish was borrowed, too, this time from our neighbors in the Orient.

MENU

FISH GONE BANANAS

POTATOES CARAWAY

TOMATO SLICES

HOT ROLLS

ICE CREAM WITH PEACH SLICES

Fish Gone Bananas

4 fish fillets
1 tablespoon butter
1 tablespoon oil
Flour seasoned with salt and pepper
2 firm bananas, quartered
¼ cup melted butter
Chopped parsley

Heat butter and oil in a skillet. Mix enough flour with salt and pepper to cover fish. Wash and dry fillets, dip in flour mixture and sauté until golden, about 4 to 5 minutes on each side. In a separate pan, fry bananas in a little butter about 3 minutes. Arrange bananas on top of fish and pour melted butter over all. Garnish with chopped parsley. Serves. 4.

Potatoes Caraway

Boil 8 small new potatoes in their jackets until tender. Salt to taste and sprinkle with about ¼ teaspoon caraway seed. Serves 4.

Tomato Slices

4 medium ripe tomatoes
Lettuce
Dressing

Core and slice tomatoes and arrange on a bed of lettuce. Sprinkle with your favorite dressing. Serves 4.

QUILTING HINT: If a very bright or dark fabric is being used in a quilt, distribute it over the whole design so the viewer's eye won't be drawn to just one section of the quilt.

Cup and Saucer

The cup in this pattern may have originally held herb tea from the garden of the woman who first stitched it. For the soup in this meal, make the cup a large one — it's so good the family will be asking for refills.

MENU
GROUND BEEF SOUP

HEARTY GREEN SALAD

TOASTED BAGELS

RICH BROWNIE CAKE

Ground Beef Soup

1 pound ground beef
2 cups mixed vegetables, from the refrigerator
  or frozen
½ cup diced celery
1 medium onion, chopped
¼ cup raw rice
2 teaspoons salt
½ teaspoon pepper
1 16-ounce can tomatoes
4 cups boiling water

Break up meat in a large kettle and brown until no longer pink. Add all other ingredients, cover, bring to a boil and simmer for 1 hour. Taste to adjust seasonings. Ladle into warmed soup cups or bowls. Serves 4-6.

Hearty Green Salad

To your favorite greens, add 1 chopped hard-cooked egg and tiny cubes of cheese. Serve with creamy French dressing.

Rich Brownie Cake

1 cup margarine
½ cup corn oil
⅞ cup water
4 tablespoons cocoa

2 cups sugar
2 cups flour
1 teaspoon soda
2 eggs, slightly beaten
½ cup buttermilk

Icing

1 stick margarine
6 tablespoons buttermilk
4 tablespoons cocoa
1 package powdered sugar
1 cup chopped nuts

Grease an 11-by-15-by-1-inch pan. Combine margarine, oil, water and cocoa in a saucepan, bring to a rapid boil. Cool. Sift sugar, flour and soda together and add to cocoa mixture. Beat in eggs and buttermilk and blend well. Pour into pan and bake at 400° for 20 minutes. Meanwhile, prepare icing. Bring margarine, buttermilk and cocoa to a boil, remove from heat and beat in powdered sugar and nuts. Spread icing on cake while hot. This cake freezes beautifully.

COOKING HINT: *When buying frozen vegetables, buy the economical large bags; thaw only what you need for each meal and keep the rest frozen.*

Album

Album is a simple nine-patch design to be treasured for its memories, since each block was done by a different quilter, with her name in the center. An Album quilt was shown to company just like a family album, bringing back past pleasures. This is a meal to bring out for company: traditional fried chicken with the trimmings and ending, of course, with Album cookies.

MENU

FRIED CHICKEN

COMPANY GREEN PEAS

BAKED SWEET POTATOES

HOT BUTTERED ROLLS

ALBUM COOKIES

Fried Chicken

2 chickens, cut in serving pieces
½ cup flour
1 teaspoon salt
⅛ teaspoon pepper
4 tablespoons shortening (half butter, half oil)
½ cup white wine, consommé or water

In a clean paper bag, mix flour, salt and pepper. Wipe chicken with a damp paper towel; shake several pieces at a time in bag to coat well. Heat shortening and brown pieces quickly. Add liquid, cover and cook for 30 to 40 minutes, turning several times. For last 10 minutes, remove lid to crisp chicken. Serves 6-8.

Company Green Peas

1 package frozen green peas
2 cups thinly sliced celery
¼ cup water
½ cup sour cream
½ teaspoon salt
½ teaspoon crushed dried rosemary
Dash garlic salt
½ cup slivered almonds

In boiling water, cook peas and celery 5 minutes. Drain. Mix sour cream, salt, rosemary and garlic salt. Put peas and celery in a warm serving dish, top with sour cream mixture and sprinkle with almonds. Serves 6.

Album Cookies

¾ cup soft shortening
1⅓ cups sugar
1 egg
2 cups flour
1 tablespoon vinegar
½ teaspoon soda
¼ teaspoon salt

Cream shortening with sugar; beat in egg. Add remaining ingredients and mix well. Roll very thin and cut with a biscuit cutter or glass. On an ungreased cookie sheet, bake at 300° for 20 minutes. When cool, use frosting or raisins to write the names of individuals across cookies, 3 or 4 each. Makes about 3½ dozen cookies.

COOKING HINT: If you buy eggs directly from a farmer, refrigerate them in the carton or in a covered container so they will retain their moisture and quality. (Most eggs from grocers have been coated for this purpose.)

Bride's Quilt

Bride's Quilt is intricate and difficult — as the showpiece in her hope chest should be. The abundance of hearts is most appropriate. This dinner is a showpiece for any bride, if she believes in the old truism about the way to a man's heart.

MENU
POACHED FRESH SALMON

EGG SAUCE (optional)

ASPARAGUS WITH BUTTERED CRUMBS

MIXED GREENS AND CUCUMBER SALAD

STRAWBERRIES

Poached Fresh Salmon with Egg Sauce

1½ pounds fresh salmon, steaks or tail piece
1 slice onion
2 teaspoons salt
1 tablespoon lemon juice

In a large skillet, combine onion, salt, lemon juice and enough water to cover fish; bring to a boil. Add salmon and bring to a boil again. Cover and simmer, allowing 10 minutes per 1 inch of fish measured at the thickest part. (For example, if fish is 1½ inches thick, simmer 15 minutes.) Serve with egg sauce. Serves 4.

Egg Sauce (optional)

2 tablespoons margarine
2 tablespoons flour
¼ teaspoon salt
Dash of pepper
1 teaspoon prepared mustard
1 cup milk
2 hard boiled eggs, sliced

Melt margarine, stir in flour, salt, pepper and mustard to make a smooth paste. Add milk, whisk until smooth and thickened. Add eggs. Keep hot in top of double boiler if prepared ahead of time. Serve over fish or pass in a bowl.

Asparagus with Buttered Crumbs

1 pound fresh asparagus
¾ cup bread crumbs
2 tablespoons butter, melted

Snap off tough lower part of stalks. Wash and trim to remove scales. Stand stalks upright in bottom of a double boiler. Add one to two inches water. Turn top of double boiler upside down to act as a cover. Cook in boiling water for 10 minutes. Toss bread crumbs in butter and serve over steamed asparagus. Serves 4.

Mixed Greens and Cucumber Salad

Wash and dry two or more varieties of lettuce. Tear into bite-size pieces, add chopped green onion and a thinly sliced cucumber. Toss with your favorite dressing.

COOKING HINT: When only a little lemon juice is needed, get a few drops by piercing a lemon with a skewer; the lemon will stay fresher than if cut.

Birds in the Air

Birds in the Air were a welcome sight to the quilter after a long and often dreary winter. Veal birds on the table are an equally pleasant sight at the end of a long winter's day.

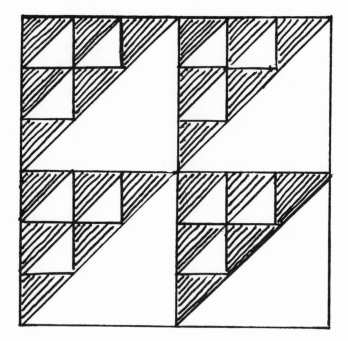

MENU
VEAL BIRDS

BOILED NEW POTATOES

PIQUANT SPINACH

HOT BUTTERED ROLLS

LEMON VELVET

Veal Birds

2 pounds veal slices from the round, ⅓ inch thick
Bacon
Flour
Oil
1 10¾-ounce can cream of mushroom soup
½ soup can water

Cut veal into 2 inch by 4 inch pieces. Roll and wrap each piece with ½ slice bacon and fasten with a toothpick. Dredge in flour and sauté slowly in hot cooking oil until golden. Transfer birds to casserole. Pour soup and ½ can water into skillet and mix well with pan drippings. Pour sauce over birds, cover and bake at 350° for 1 hour. Add water as needed to keep good gravy consistency. Serves 6.

Piquant Spinach

3 packages frozen chopped spinach
1 small onion, chopped
1 tablespoon butter
2 tablespoons lemon juice

Cook spinach according to package directions; drain well. Sauté onions in butter, add lemon juice and pour over hot spinach. Serves 6.

Lemon Velvet

2½ cups lemon pie filling
1 7-ounce jar marshmallow fluff
1 cup heavy cream, whipped

Combine all ingredients and mix with electric beater at low speed. Pour into dish or ice trays and freeze until firm. To serve, spoon into wine glasses. Serves 6.

COOKING HINT: *Vary cooked potatoes with a sprinkling of herbs such as savory, basil, rosemary or dill.*

Chinese Puzzle

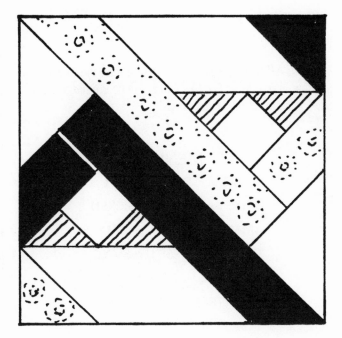

Chinese Puzzle looks like — and may well have been copied from — the puzzles made from squares of wood cut into intricate shapes, and nearly impossible to put together. Not so this meal — it is easy to put together and, though Oriental in origin, it's no puzzle.

MENU
MARINATED FLANK STEAK

SKILLET-BROWNED POTATOES

PEAS WITH WATER CHESTNUTS

CHOCOLATE CHIP COOKIES

Marinated Flank Steak

To be prepared a day in advance.

1 flank steak, 1 to 2 pounds
¼ cup soy sauce
¾ cup oil
3 tablespoons honey
2 tablespoons vinegar
1½ teaspoons each garlic and fresh gingeroot, chopped
2 green onions, chopped

Put flank steak in a large, shallow glass dish. Mix remaining ingredients and pour over steak. Cover and store in refrigerator overnight, turning steak once to marinate both sides. Broil 4 to 5 minutes on each side. To serve, cut thin slices on the bias. Serves 4.

Skillet-Browned Potatoes

1 pound small white potatoes
2 tablespoons butter

Boil potatoes in skins until tender, cool and peel. Melt butter in large skillet; sauté potatoes in a single layer until golden brown on all sides. Serves 4.

Peas with Water Chestnuts

1 package frozen peas
4 canned water chestnuts, sliced thin

Prepare peas according to directions on package. Add water chestnuts; heat for 1 or 2 minutes; drain. Serves 4.

COOKING HINT: Line pans used for broiling or roasting meat or fish with foil to eliminate the messy job of scouring the pans. Don't do this, however, if gravy is to be made from the meat drippings — gravy-making cleans the pan.

Hands All Around

Hands All Around reflects a group of quilters busily working together at a quilting bee. All hands will be around this salad bowl, each fixing his or her own.

MENU
CHEESE-GRAPE PLATTER

DAD'S BAR-B-QUED CHICKEN

MAKE-YOUR-OWN SALAD

GREEN GODDESS DRESSING

POTATO OR MACARONI SALAD

BUTTERED SOFT ROLLS

WATERMELON

Cheese-Grape Platter

On a large platter, arrange an assortment of 3 or 4 different cheeses, such as Tilsit, jack, Gruyère, cheddar or Edam, cut in 1-inch cubes. Ring the cheese with several kinds of cocktail crackers. In center of platter, put several bunches of chilled, sweet grapes.

Dad's Bar-B-Qued Chicken

3 chickens, quartered
Barbeque sauce (recipe below)

Broil chicken over hot coals about 10 minutes on each side. Put leg and thigh quarters in the hottest place on the grill. Brush upper side with barbeque sauce, turn and broil for about 4 minutes (do not let the sauce burn). Repeat for the other side, and continue turning until chicken is done. Remove from heat and serve at once. Serves 8-12.

Barbeque Sauce

1 cup ketchup or tomato sauce
½ cup water
½ cup vinegar
1 small onion, minced
1 clove garlic, pressed
½ teaspoon celery seed
1 tablespoon brown sugar
2 teaspoons dry mustard
½ to 2 teaspoons each chili powder and cumin (depending on taste)

Mix ingredients in a saucepan and simmer for 15 minutes. Cool. Whirl in a blender until smooth. Makes about 2 cups.

Make-Your-Own Salad

1 head iceberg lettuce
1 head romaine
1 basket cherry tomatoes
1 cucumber, thinly sliced
1 green pepper, cut in thin rings
½ cup chopped green onion
1 large bunch radishes
½ pound fresh mushrooms, sliced
Croutons

Wash lettuce and pat dry. Tear into bite-sized pieces and put in a large serving bowl. Place remaining ingredients in separate bowls. To serve, surround lettuce with salad trimmings and let guests make their own salads, and pass bottled green goddess dressing.

QUILTING HINT: When a quilt has several borders, the outside border should usually be the darkest color since it "frames" the quilt.

Farmer's Daughter

Maybe the Farmer's Daughter was created by a farmer's daughter as she sat on a haystack enjoying the sun. These haystacks have never seen a farm, but they are tasty cookies.

MENU

ENGLISH HOTPOT OF BEEF

BUTTERED NOODLES

HONEY-GLAZED CARROTS

TOSSED GREEN SALAD WITH CHERRY TOMATOES

HAYSTACKS

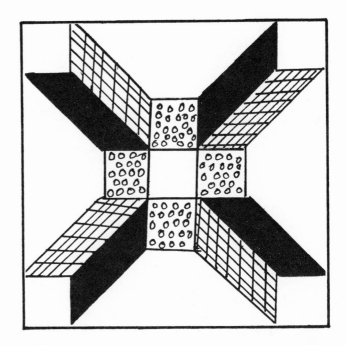

English Hotpot of Beef

1½ *pounds beef, cut in 1-inch cubes*
2½ *cups boiling water*
2 *tablespoons chopped onion*
2 *cloves garlic, minced*
1 *teaspoon salt*
¼ *teaspoon pepper*
¼ *teaspoon paprika*
Dash of allspice
1 *teaspoon sugar*
2 *teaspoons lemon juice*
1 *teaspoon Worcestershire sauce*
⅓ *cup tomato juice*
½ *cup sliced carrots*
1 *cup cubed potatoes*
½ *cup diced celery*
1 *cup frozen pearl onions*

Shake meat in a paper bag with flour. Brown in a little hot fat. Add boiling water, onion, garlic, seasonings, lemon juice, Worcestershire sauce and tomato juice. Cover tightly and simmer 2 hours or until meat is tender. Add vegetables; continue cooking about 30 minutes or until vegetables are done. Serves 6.

Honey-Glazed Carrots

8-10 *carrots, sliced thin*
¼ *cup butter*
2 *teaspoons honey*

Cook carrots in a little water for about 10 minutes. Watch carefully that they don't overcook. Drain. Melt butter with honey, add carrots and heat slowly until carrot slices are glazed. Serves 6.

Haystacks

1 *egg white*
½ *cup sugar*
½ *teaspoon allspice*
½ *teaspoon cinnamon*
1 *cup broken pretzels*
2 *cups peanuts*

Beat egg white until soft peaks form. Add sugar and spices gradually. Continue beating until very stiff. Fold in pretzels and peanuts. Drop in small "haystacks" on greased cookie sheet. Bake at 325° for 20 minutes or until lightly browned. Makes 4 dozen.

COOKING HINT: *Extra egg yolks can usually be substituted for whole eggs in baking custards — use two yolks for each whole egg required. Leftover yolks may be poached until solid and used to garnish salads or sandwiches.*

Rail Fence

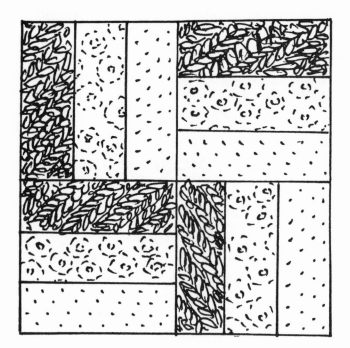

Rail Fence is simple and geometric. Its color arrangement gives the impression of an old split-rail fence — perhaps the fence that kept our lamb from straying.

MENU
CURRIED LAMBBURGERS ON BUNS

FRESH VEGETABLE SALAD

STUFFED CINNAMON PEARS

Curried Lambburgers on Buns

1 pound ground lamb
Onion salt and garlic salt
¼ cup margarine
¾ teaspoon curry powder
4 hamburger buns

Shape lamb into four patties. Sprinkle both sides with onion salt and garlic salt to taste. Cook in broiler or on barbecue 15 to 20 minutes, turning once, until well browned on both sides. Melt margarine with curry powder and spread on both sides of cooked patties. Serve on warmed buns. Serves 4.

Fresh Vegetable Salad

Chop an assortment of fresh vegetables — zucchini, carrots, celery, green onions, radishes, green pepper or yellow crookneck squash. Toss with French dressing and marinate several hours or all day.

Stuffed Cinnamon Pears

2 3-ounce packages cream cheese
1 small wedge bleu cheese (about 2 ounces)
2 tablespoons milk
⅛ teaspoon salt
Dash of pepper
¼ teaspoon cinnamon
4 ripe pears

In a blender or with a beater, mix cheeses, milk, salt, pepper and cinnamon until fluffy. Cut unpeeled pears in half and remove cores. Brush tops with lemon juice to prevent discoloration. Fill cavities with cheese mixture. Serves 4.

QUILTING HINT: *Square or rectangular pattern pieces should be placed on the straight of the material.*

Hovering Hawks

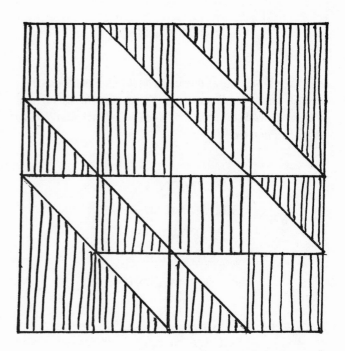

Hovering Hawks were an almost perpetual sight from the farmhouse of a hundred years ago. This is a relatively easy pattern to piece despite the number of patches. The menu, too, is easy to put together, despite the number of ingredients in the minestrone.

MENU
MELON SLICES WITH HAM

MINESTRONE

SESAME SLICES

LEMON CUSTARD ICE CREAM

Melon Slices with Ham

1 cantaloupe or honeydew melon
¼ pound thinly sliced boiled ham or prosciutto
Lettuce leaves

Slice melon in 16 segments, remove rind. Wrap a piece of ham around each segment. Arrange on lettuce leaves. Serves 8.

Minestrone

⅓ cup oil
2-3 medium onions, chopped
2 celery stalks with tops, chopped
2 tablespoons chopped parsley
1 6-ounce can tomato paste
2 10½-ounce cans beef broth
8 cups water
2 or 3 beef bouillon cubes
2 carrots, sliced
2 teaspoons salt
¼ teaspoon pepper
½ teaspoon sage
½ teaspoon rosemary
1 1-pound can kidney beans, drained
1 medium zucchini, sliced
1 package frozen cut green beans
¼ to ½ head cabbage, shredded
1 cup elbow macaroni
3 sweet Italian sausages, sliced (optional)
Grated Parmesan cheese

Heat oil; add onions, celery and parsley, sauté until tender. Stir in tomato paste, beef broth, water, bouillon cubes, carrots, salt, pepper, sage and rosemary. Bring to boil. Simmer, covered, for 45 minutes. (Note: soup may be prepared to this point in advance. Store in refrigerator and reheat to boiling.) Add kidney beans, remaining vegetables, macaroni and sausage, cooking over low heat for 20 minutes. Ladle into warmed soup bowls and sprinkle with Parmesan cheese. Serves 6-8.

Sesame Slices

1 loaf Italian or sweet French bread
½ cup melted butter or margarine
2 tablespoons sesame seeds

Cut bread into slices almost to bottom crust. Brush each slice with butter and sprinkle with sesame seeds. Wrap in foil and heat at 400° for 10 minutes or until well heated. Serve warm.

QUILTING HINT: Keep fabric pieces laid out in the shape of the pattern while sewing to avoid errors.

Broken Dishes

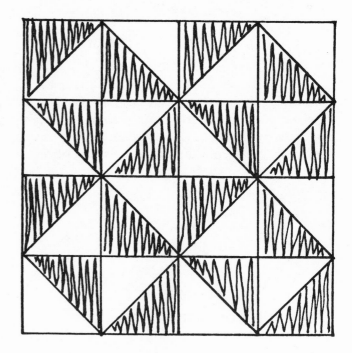

Broken Dishes shows the shards on the kitchen floor after an accident caused by slippery soap. We are sure this would have to be explained to the competent and efficient cook who'll make this Oriental menu!

MENU

TERIYAKI STEAK STRIPS

SNOW PEAS

STEAMED RICE

GINGERED MELON BALLS

Teriyaki Steak Strips

2-pound flank steak
1 cup consommé (or ½ cup consommé and
    ½ cup red wine)
⅓ cup soy sauce
1½ teaspoons seasoned salt
¼ cup chopped green onion
1 clove garlic, minced
3 tablespoons lime juice
2 tablespoons sugar

Cut meat diagonally into 1-inch strips. Mix remaining ingredients, pour over meat, cover and marinate overnight. Broil quickly over charcoal or in the broiler, about 2 minutes on each side. Serves 4-6.

Snow Peas

Prepare frozen snow peas according to directions on package, or cook fresh snow peas in ¼ cup boiling water until they turn bright green, about 5 minutes. Dot with butter and serve hot. Serves 4-6.

Gingered Melon Balls

3 cups melon balls (honeydew, cantaloupe, Crenshaw, casaba)
1½ tablespoons honey
¼ cup finely chopped crystallized ginger

Combine melon balls, honey and ginger. Chill until ready to serve. Serves 6.

COOKING HINT: *Pick up slivers of glass or crockery with a wet paper towel and there'll be no blood on the tiles.*

Brunswick Star

Brunswick Star, Rolling Star or Chained Star are all appropriate names for this block, one of the hundreds of star patterns found in quilts. There are more than twenty Brunswick placenames in the world, not counting the ''New'' or ''East'' or ''South'' Brunswicks; there are at least as many well-known chicken stews, but none better than this Brunswick Stew.

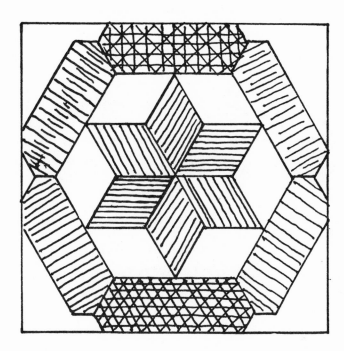

MENU
BRUNSWICK STEW

HOT CRUSTY BREAD

FRESH GREENS WITH SESAME DRESSING

LEMON PIE

Brunswick Stew

1 3½-pound chicken, cut in pieces
1½ cups canned tomatoes
½ cup chopped onion
1 cup frozen or fresh lima beans
3 potatoes, diced
1 tablespoon sugar
Salt and pepper
1 cup whole kernel corn
1 teaspoon Worcestershire sauce

In a large pot, cover chicken pieces with boiling water. Cover and simmer until tender, 1 to 1½ hours. Take out the chicken pieces, remove meat from bones and cut into small pieces. Return chicken to pot and add tomatoes, onions, lima beans, potatoes, sugar and salt and pepper to taste. Cook until lima beans and potatoes are tender. Add corn and Worcestershire sauce and cook 5 minutes longer. Serves 6.

Sesame Dressing

⅔ cup oil
2 tablespoons vinegar
2 tablespoons toasted sesame seeds
1 tablespoon sugar
½ teaspoon salt
¼ teaspoon pepper

Mix all ingredients in a covered jar and shake well. Just before serving, pour over fresh, crisp salad greens. Makes one cup.

Lemon Pie

1 cup sugar
2 heaping tablespoons flour
2 tablespoons melted butter
2 large egg yolks
Pinch salt
Grated rind and juice of 2 lemons
1¼ cups milk
2 egg whites, stiffly beaten
1 unbaked pie shell

Beat together first 5 ingredients until creamy. Add grated rind and juice of lemons. Blend well. Add milk and fold in egg whites. Pour into unbaked pie shell and bake at 325° for about 45 minutes.

COOKING HINT: ''Beat until stiff but not dry'' means beating egg whites until they just stay in the bowl when it is held upside down.

Maple Leaf

Maple Leaf is the name of several block patterns in addition to this one. There are also Palm Leaves, Oak Leaves, a Tulip Tree Leaf, a Buckeye Leaf, a Poplar Leaf and more. While there are as many meat loaf recipes as there are cooks, the spicy barbeque taste of this one is special.

MENU

BARBEQUED MEAT LOAVES

LETTUCE WEDGES

POTATOES IN A TENT

MAPLE PARFAITS

Barbequed Meat Loaves

1½ pounds ground beef
½ pound ground lean pork
3-4 slices bacon, diced
½ cup evaporated milk
1 egg, lightly beaten
2 teaspoons salt
1 cup coarse bread crumbs, fresh or dry
2 teaspoons chopped onion
½ cup ketchup
½ cup vinegar
1 tablespoon Worcestershire sauce
1 teaspoon chili powder

Mix ground beef, ground pork, bacon, milk, egg, salt, bread crumbs and onion together well. Shape into 8 small loaves and place in a baking dish. Combine ketchup, vinegar, Worcestershire sauce and chili powder in a saucepan, bring to a boil and simmer 5 to 10 minutes. Pour over loaves and bake at 350° for 1 hour. Baste often or cover with foil. Serves 8.

Potatoes in a Tent

8 potatoes, peeled
½ cup grated cheese
½ cup light cream
3 tablespoons butter
2 tablespoons chopped parsley
Salt and pepper to taste

Cut the potatoes as for french fries and place on a piece of heavy foil. Combine cheese and cream and pour over potatoes, dot with butter, add parsley and season to taste. Fold foil in tent fashion, being sure to seal edges tightly. Bake at 350° for 45 minutes. Serves 8.

Maple Parfaits

1 quart vanilla ice cream
Maple syrup
½ cup chopped walnuts or pecans

In 8 parfait glasses, alternate ice cream and syrup until glass is full, ending with syrup. Sprinkle nuts on top.

QUILTING HINT: Quilt block squares are usually designed to be from 6 to 12 inches, but can be as large as 16 inches square. The larger the square, the fewer needed for a quilt.

The Ship

This pattern, The Ship, could easily be a fishing vessel going out for a load of salmon. But it won't be as high in the water when it comes home loaded with the fishermen's catch.

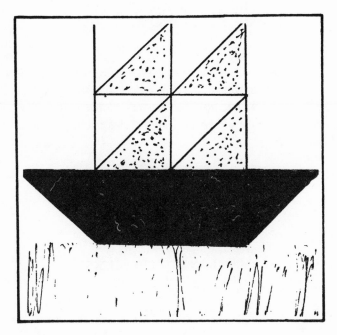

MENU
BAKED SALMON LOAF

CORN NIBLETS

BROCCOLI VINAIGRETTE

PRUNE WHIP

Baked Salmon Loaf

1 1-pound can salmon
Milk
1½ cups soft bread crumbs
2 tablespoons chopped parsley
½ teaspoon salt
Dash of pepper
Dash of garlic powder
2 eggs

Drain juice from canned salmon into a measuring cup and add enough milk to make 1 cup. Break up salmon with a fork, discarding any large bones. Combine fish with crumbs, parsley, salt, pepper and garlic powder. Beat eggs with milk and mix with salmon. Bake in greased loaf pan at 350° for 40 minutes. Serves 6.

Corn Niblets

2 tablespoons butter
2 tablespoons minced onion
3 tablespoons minced green pepper
2 12-ounce cans corn niblets, drained
Salt and pepper
1 teaspoon sugar

Melt butter and sauté onions and green pepper. Add corn, salt, pepper and sugar and heat through. Serves 6.

Broccoli Vinaigrette

Marinate cooked broccoli stalks in French dressing for several hours. Serve on salad plates.

Prune Whip

½ cup heavy cream
1 tablespoon sugar
2 4¾-ounce jars strained baby food prunes,
  or 1 each of prunes and apricots

Whip cream with sugar until stiff. Gently fold in prunes and chill until serving time. Serve in small dessert dishes. Serves 6.

COOKING HINT: To cut butter cleanly without broken edges, cover the knife with a piece of waxed paper, or use a warm knife.

Children's Delight

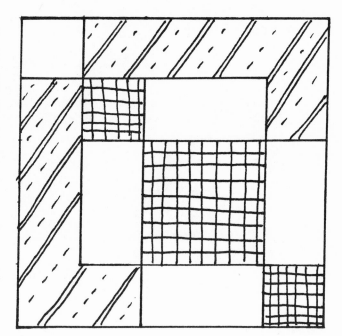

Children's Delight had to have been called that because it was so simple and the patches were large; it was an ideal pattern for the little girl's first quilt. This menu of chicken, buttered rice and pumpkin pie will be the delight of children from three to sixty-three.

MENU

CHICKEN PAPRIKA

BUTTERED RICE

CARROT AND CELERY STICKS

WARM RYE BREAD SLICES

PUMPKIN PIE

Chicken Paprika

2 chickens, cut in pieces
½ cup flour
2 teaspoons salt
¼ teaspoon pepper
1 teaspoon paprika
½ cup butter (or half butter and half cooking oil)
2 cups chicken stock or water
1 pint sour cream, divided
1 grated onion
2 tablespoons chili sauce
1 tablespoon Worcestershire sauce

Dredge chicken pieces in flour mixed with salt, pepper and paprika. Brown in butter. Add stock, half of the sour cream, onion, chili sauce and Worcestershire sauce. Cover and cook 1½ hours. Skim off excess fat and add remaining sour cream. Thicken juices with a bit of flour and water shaken together if necessary. Serve on a bed of rice. Serves 6.

Pumpkin Pie

2 eggs, beaten
2 cups evaporated milk
1 cup canned pumpkin
2 tablespoons cornstarch
¼ cup sugar
1 teaspoon cinnamon
Pinch of salt
1 baked pie shell

Mix eggs, milk and pumpkin together in a saucepan. Stir dry ingredients together, add to pumpkin mixture and cook over low heat until thick and bubbly. Cool and spoon into baked pie shell. Chill and serve. Serves 6.

COOKING HINT: *Reduce chicken stock to one-fourth of the original volume and freeze into ¼-cup cubes. Then, one cube plus ¾ cup water will equal a cup of stock. Be sure to skim off all the fat before freezing. (Save the fat for cooking.)*

Double Irish Chain

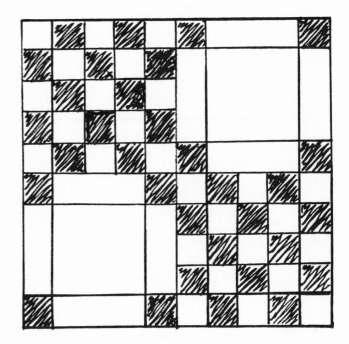

Double Irish Chain is a spectacular all-over pattern for a quilt, although the checkerboard or confetti effect of a single block is not as pronounced. If green noodles were used instead of spaghetti in this recipe — as they well could be — it could be renamed Irish Confetti.

MENU

CLAM CONFETTI SPAGHETTI

FRESH MUSHROOM SALAD

BLUEBERRIES WITH CREAM

Clam Confetti Spaghetti

2 tablespoons olive oil
1 onion, chopped
½ green pepper, chopped
3 cloves garlic
1 1-lb can Italian peeled tomatoes
1 6½-ounce can minced clams
½ cup chopped parsley
Spaghetti

In olive oil sauté onion, green pepper and garlic until soft. Add tomatoes and simmer for 10 minutes or until the sauce has been reduced a bit. Add clams and parsley. Sauce is ready as soon as it is heated through. Pour it over cooked spaghetti. Serves 2-3.

Fresh Mushroom Salad

1 package frozen petit peas
½ cup vinaigrette dressing, divided
⅓ pound mushrooms, sliced
½ cup finely chopped celery

Cook peas according to package directions, adding ½ teaspoon sugar to water. Pour half the dressing over drained hot peas. Let cool. Add mushrooms and celery. Toss gently with remaining dressing. Serves 4.

Blueberries with Cream

1 package fresh or frozen blueberries
Confectioners sugar
Sweet cream or dairy sour cream

Sprinkle berries with sugar. Pass cream in separate pitcher or bowl. Serves 4.

QUILTING HINT: Quilting patterns show up best on a plain-colored backing. However, figured backing hides unevenness in stitches.

Grape Basket

Grape Basket is one of the dozens of baskets appearing in quilt designs. This one holds the chilled grapes that are just the right finish for this dinner of pizza and Caesar salad.

MENU
PITA PIZZA
CAESAR SALAD
CHILLED GRAPES

Pita Pizza

6 pita (pocket) breads
1 11-ounce jar meatless spaghetti sauce
4 medium tomatoes, sliced
1 can anchovy fillets, drained
½ pound fresh mushrooms, sliced
8 ounces pepperoni or Italian salami, sliced
½ pound mozzarella cheese, grated

Spoon spaghetti sauce over the top of each pita bread. Set out remaining ingredients in individual bowls and let everyone decorate his or her own pizza. Place pizzas on a large cookie sheet and bake at 375° until cheese is melted, about 10 to 15 minutes. Makes 6 servings.

Caesar Salad

1 clove garlic
4 tablespoons salad oil
1½ tablespoons lemon juice
1 teaspoon Worcestershire sauce
½ teaspoon salt
1 head romaine
4 anchovy fillets, chopped
1 egg, boiled for 1 minute
½ cup Parmesan cheese
½ to ¾ cup croutons

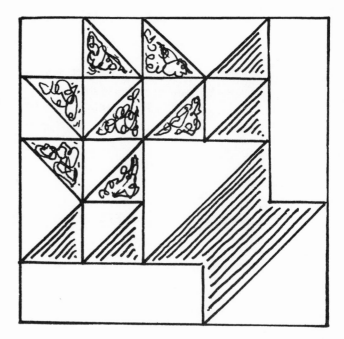

Rub the inside of a wooden salad bowl with the garlic. Combine oil, lemon juice, Worcestershire sauce and salt in the bowl and mix with a wooden spoon until well blended. Tear lettuce into bite-sized pieces and add to bowl. Add the anchovies and break the egg over the salad. Mix well. Sprinkle with Parmesan cheese and croutons and mix well again. Serve at once. Serves 6.

QUILTING HINT: A *single quilt block can be padded, backed and bound to make a hot pad for protecting a table surface.*

House on a Hill

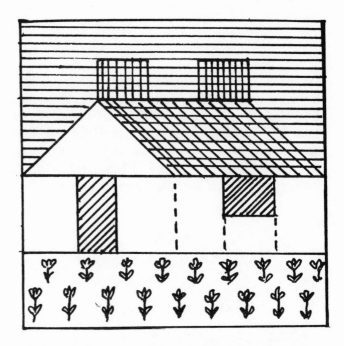

Once upon a time there was a House on a Hill, and in that house were a man and his wife and four small children. They had all just finished eating a lovely meal of beef tenderloin and potato puffs and orange and avocado salad and were stuffing their mouths with chocolate mousse. And they were saying, through the chocolate, "What a nice, hard-working mother we have to spend all day making such an elegant meal," and the mother was just smiling, thinking of the quilt she had worked on that day.

MENU

TENDERLOIN OF BEEF

POTATO PUFFS

BED OF LETTUCE WITH ORANGE AND
AVOCADO SLICES

HOT ROLLS

CHOCOLATE MOUSSE

Tenderloin of Beef

1 4-to-5-pound beef tenderloin
½ stick butter or margarine, melted
½ cup Worcestershire sauce
1 can mushroom stems and pieces, drained
Flour and water

Place a large piece of heavy foil in a roasting pan. Put beef on foil and pour over melted butter and Worcestershire sauce. Marinate for two hours. Wrap foil tightly around meat and bake at 350° for 1 hour. Open foil, add mushrooms and baste meat. Continue cooking for ½ hour with foil open so that meat can brown. Remove to warm platter and thicken juices with flour and water if gravy is desired. Slice thin. Serves 6, with leftovers.

Potato Puffs

2 eggs, separated
1 cup riced boiled potatoes
1 cup flour
1 teaspoon baking powder
1 cup milk
Salt
Shortening

Lightly beat egg yolks and add to potatoes. Sift flour and baking powder together and add, alternating with milk, to potatoes. Beat egg whites until stiff and fold into mixture. Salt to taste. Put 1½ inches shortening into a medium-sized heavy saucepan and heat until sizzling. Drop small portions of potato mixture, a few at a time, from a teaspoon into hot fat. Cook until puffed and delicately browned. Drain on paper towels and keep warm in oven. Serves 6.

Chocolate Mousse

½ pound sweet chocolate
Boiling water
6 tablespoons powdered sugar
6 eggs, separated
Whipped cream

Break chocolate into small pieces. Place in bowl and just cover with boiling water. Cover bowl and let stand 5 minutes. Carefully pour off water. Stir chocolate with a fork while adding sugar gradually. Beat egg yolks slightly and stir into chocolate. Beat egg whites very stiff and fold into chocolate mixture. Pour into individual dishes, cups or serving dish. Refrigerate for 8 hours or overnight. To serve, top with a dollop of whipped cream. Serves 6.

QUILTING HINT: In quilting, eight stitches per inch are considered about right.

Log Cabin

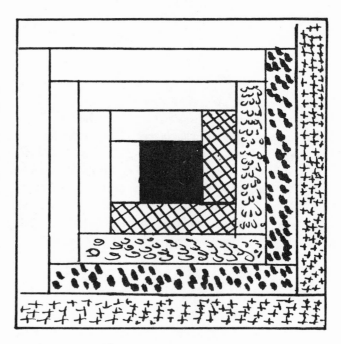

Log Cabin, a favorite design of quilters, can be made into a number of different all-over patterns by varying the way the basic blocks are placed and by different color arrangements. Barn Raising, Courthouse Steps, Windmill Blades and Pineapple are a few of the variations. There are few dishes more traditional and favorite than spareribs and sauerkraut — and the pineapple in the salad comes right from this quilt block.

MENU

SPARERIBS AND SAUERKRAUT

MASHED POTATOES

BEETS AND PINEAPPLE

GINGERBREAD

Spareribs and Sauerkraut

3 pounds spareribs
Salt and pepper
2 1-pound cans Bavarian-style sauerkraut
½ teaspoon caraway seeds

In a heavy skillet, brown the spareribs, seasoned with salt and pepper. In an ovenproof dish, spread sauerkraut, sprinkle with caraway seeds and place meat over sauerkraut. Add ½ cup hot water, cover tightly and bake at 350° for 1½ to 2 hours. Serves 4-6.

Beets and Pineapple

1 #2 can pineapple chunks
2 tablespoons cornstarch
1 #303 can diced or julienne beets
1 tablespoon vinegar
¾ teaspoon salt

Drain pineapple chunks, reserving juice. Blend 2 tablespoons pineapple juice with cornstarch. Drain beets, reserving liquid. In a saucepan, combine reserved juice and beet liquid with cornstarch mixture. Heat, stirring constantly, until thickened. Add vinegar, salt, pineapple chunks and beets and heat through. Serves 4-6.

Gingerbread

This recipe makes a lot, but it keeps well.

1 cup unsulphured molasses
1½ cups hot milk
1 teaspoon baking soda
½ cup butter
1 cup sugar
½ teaspoon salt
1 teaspoon ginger
2 teaspoons cinnamon
1 egg, beaten
2½ cups flour
1 tablespoon baking powder

Combine molasses with hot milk and soda; cool mixture. Cream butter with sugar. Add molasses mixture, salt, ginger and cinnamon and beat well. Add egg; sift flour with baking powder and add. Pour into two greased 7-by-11-inch pans. Bake at 375° for 20 minutes; reduce heat to 300° and bake for 20 minutes more. Serve warm with applesauce or ice cream.

QUILTING HINT: Don't fret if your quilting results are not perfect. The charm of handmade things is a bit of irregularity. Old quilts often have a deliberate mistake pieced into them lest ''perfection'' offend the Lord.

Winged Square

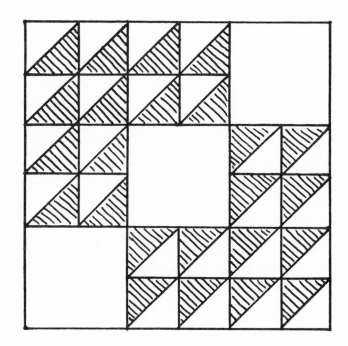

Winged Square looks very much like a pre-Columbian Indian picture of an owl flying overhead. The designer of this block could easily have had in mind the flapping wings of the young rooster which was about to become oven-fried chicken.

MENU

OVEN-FRIED CHICKEN WITH
LEMON BARBEQUE SAUCE

BERMUDA SALAD BOWL

HOT ROLLS OR BISCUITS

BAKED BANANAS WITH MARMALADE

Oven-Fried Chicken with Lemon Barbeque Sauce

1 chicken, cut in serving pieces
¼ cup butter
½ cup flour
1 teaspoon salt
¼ teaspoon pepper
2 teaspoons paprika

Lemon Barbeque Sauce

1 clove garlic
½ teaspoon salt
¼ cup oil
½ cup lemon juice
2 tablespoons chopped onion
½ teaspoon each pepper and ground thyme

Melt butter in a shallow baking dish in 400° oven. Mix flour, salt, pepper and paprika in a clean paper bag. Place chicken pieces, a few at a time, in the bag and shake to coat. Put chicken in baking dish, turning to coat with butter. Bake skin side down in a single layer, uncovered, at 400° for 30 minutes. Meanwhile, make barbeque sauce: mash garlic with salt, add remaining ingredients and mix well. Turn chicken skin side up and pour sauce over all. Bake 30 minutes longer or until tender. Serves 4-6.

Bermuda Salad Bowl

1 small head cauliflower
½ large mild onion
½ cup stuffed olives
⅔ cup French dressing
½ head lettuce, shredded
½ cup crumbled Roquefort cheese

Break cauliflower into florets and slice florets crosswise into thin slices. Slice onion crosswise and chop coarsely. Slice olives. Marinate all in French dressing for half an hour. Just before serving, add shredded lettuce and cheese. Toss together in a salad bowl until the lettuce is thoroughly coated with dressing. Serves 4-6.

Baked Bananas with Marmalade

4 bananas
Margarine
Marmalade
Chopped almonds

Peel and slice bananas lengthwise. Place flat side up in a baking dish coated with margarine. Spread marmalade generously over bananas and sprinkle with almonds. Bake at 375° for 10 minutes. Serve at once. Serves 4.

QUILTING HINT: Always wash and iron fabric before using it to eliminate shrinkage and test for colorfastness.

Garden of Eden

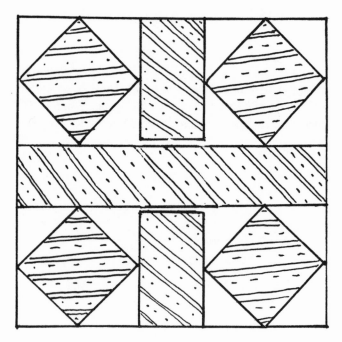

Garden of Eden is a simple pattern, and a bold design when made with constrasting colors. The best greens for the salad for this meal would come straight from the garden, with no snake to fear.

MENU
BEEF-BARLEY SOUP/STEW

POPPY-SEED BREAD

CRISP GREEN SALAD

DROP SUGAR COOKIES

Beef-Barley Soup/Stew

1 pound ground beef
1 large onion, chopped
3 stalks celery, sliced
3 carrots, sliced
½ cup barley
1 single-serving package dry tomato soup mix
4 beef bouillon cubes
5 cups water
2 teaspoons chili powder
Salt and pepper

In a large pot, crumble and cook beef until brown. Add onion, celery and carrots; cook until vegetables are limp. Add barley, tomato soup mix, bouillon cubes, water and chili powder. Cover and simmer 45 to 50 minutes. Salt and pepper to taste. Serves 4-6.

Poppy-Seed Bread

1 loaf crusty bread
1 stick butter or margarine
2 tablespoons poppy seeds

Cut bread in slices almost to the bottom crust. Spread each slice with butter and sprinkle with poppy seeds. Wrap in foil and heat at 400° for 10 minutes or until well heated. Serve warm.

Drop Sugar Cookies

2 eggs
⅔ cup cooking oil
2 teaspoons vanilla
1 teaspoon lemon rind, grated
¾ cup sugar
2 cups flour
2 teaspoons baking powder
½ teaspoon salt
Pecan halves

In a mixing bowl, beat eggs, oil, vanilla and lemon rind. Beat in sugar until mixture thickens. Sift flour, baking powder and salt together. Blend into egg mixture. Drop by teaspoonfuls on ungreased baking sheet, 1 inch apart. Press a pecan half into top of each cookie. Bake at 325° for 8-10 minutes.

COOKING HINT: Washed salad greens wrapped in paper towels and refrigerated for an hour or so will be deliciously crisp when served.

Storm at Sea

Storm at Sea has squares and diamonds of different sizes and shapes — like wind-tossed waves. Quilters have seen many different things in this design: it has at least thirteen different names. There are many more than thirteen different species in the salmon family — but one must be caught before the storm comes.

MENU
SALMON MOUSSE

NEW POTATOES WITH PARSLEY BUTTER

GREEN PEAS

FRESH PINEAPPLE TIDBITS

Salmon Mousse

1 envelope unflavored gelatin
2 tablespoons lemon juice
2 teaspoons dried minced onion or 1 small onion, sliced
½ cup boiling water
½ cup mayonnaise
¼ teaspoon paprika
1 teaspoon dried dill
1 1-pound can salmon, drained
1 cup half and half

Put gelain, lemon juice, onion and boiling water in a blender, cover, and blend on high speed for 30 seconds. Add mayonnaise, paprika, dill and salmon and blend for 10 seconds. Gradually add half and half and blend for 30 seconds (longer blending could cause cream to curdle). Pour into a lightly oiled mold and chill until firm. Unmold to serve. Serves 4-6.

New Potatoes with Parsley Butter

6-8 small new potatoes
2 tablespoons butter
1 tablespoon minced parsley

Scrub potatoes and cook, in their jackets, about 20 minutes or until tender. Melt butter, add parsley and pour over hot potatoes. Serves 4.

Fresh Pineapple Tidbits

Peel a fresh, ripe pineapple. Cut into quarters and remove core. Cut sections into bite-sized pieces and arrange on individual serving plates. Turn a tablespoon of firmly packed brown sugar onto each plate. Dip tidbits in sugar before eating.

QUILTING HINT: Make a small ironing board by wrapping a piece of plywood with a piece of an old mattress pad and covering it with sheeting. When this board is on a small table or stool by the sewing machine, pressing small pieces becomes easy.

Corn and Beans

Corn and Beans was named by someone who could see a similarity between this pattern and the rows of sweet corn with bean vines planted below, as they used to be grown. The corn and beans come back together in this quick casserole.

MENU
BROWNED SAUSAGES

CORN AND BEAN CASSEROLE

PARKER HOUSE ROLLS

PEANUT BUTTER COOKIES

Browned Sausages

In a skillet, cook one pound of sausages (garlic, Polish, bratwurst or links) until evenly browned. Drain fat, if necessary, and continue cooking until sausages are done. Serves 4.

Corn and Bean Casserole

1 cup cooked corn
1 cup red kidney beans, drained
1 cup canned tomatoes, drained
½ teaspoon salt
¼ teaspoon paprika
1 teaspoon grated onion
1 tablespoon brown sugar

Combine all ingredients and put in a greased baking dish. Top with bread crumbs and bake, covered, at 350° for 30 to 40 minutes. Serves 4.

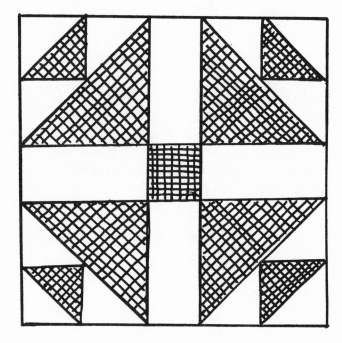

QUILTING HINT: Crazy quilts are usually just lined and bound. Rarely does one have a filler.

Puss in the Corner

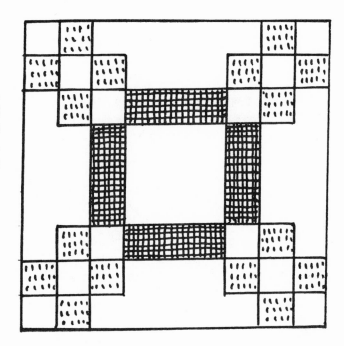

Puss in the Corner is a game that most of us have forgotten, along with Red Rover, jacks, skip-rope and a lot of others that required invention rather than batteries. The inventor of this pattern saw a cat's face in the squares in the corners of the block, just as we see sailing ships and sunsets in our doodles, when others just see squiggles.

MENU

NOODLE DOODLE

WARM ITALIAN BREAD

RADISH ROSES AND GREEN ONIONS

SHERBET IN ORANGE SHELLS

Noodle Doodle

1 pound lean beef
½ pound pork
Margarine
2 cups onions, chopped
4 stalks celery, chopped
1 green pepper, chopped
1 pound sharp cheese
2 10¾-ounce cans tomato soup, undiluted
1 8-ounce can mushroom stems and pieces
1 12-ounce package wide noodles

Have butcher grind beef and pork together. Brown meat in a little margarine. Add onions, celery and pepper and cook a few minutes longer. In a saucepan, melt cheese in tomato soup. Add soup and mushrooms to meat mixture and simmer for ½ hour. Cook noodles in salted water according to package directions. Put noodles in an ovenproof dish, mix in meat sauce and bake at 325° for 1 hour. Serves 8-10.

Radish Roses and Green Onions

1 bunch radishes
1 bunch green onions

Wash and dry radishes. Cut "petals" halfway through each radish on all four sides. Cut green onions in 4-inch strips lengthwise. Arrange on a small serving dish, cover and chill until serving time.

Sherbet in Orange Shells

Save orange shells, cleaned of pulp, in a plastic bag in the refrigerator. Fill with a scoop of orange sherbet or frozen yogurt.

COOKING HINT: If you place oranges in a hot oven for 3 to 5 minutes before peeling, little of the white fiber will remain on the oranges when you peel them.

57

Goose in the Pond

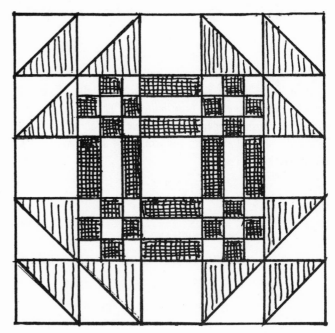

Goose in the Pond is also kr wn as Young Man's Fancy. A goose in the pond is just a step away from being this goose in the oven.

MENU

ROASTED GOOSE

ZUCCHINI CASSEROLE

WILD RICE

SESAME-SEED ROLLS

LEMON PIE FROM THE BAKERY

Roasted Goose

1 8-pound goose
1 or 2 apples, sliced (optional)
1 or 2 onions, sliced (optional)
Celery leaves (optional)
2 10¾-ounce cans consommé
2 cans water
1 can sherry
Salt and pepper

Preheat oven to 450°. Place goose on a rack, breast side up, in a roaster. Place the apple and onion slices and/or celery tops in cavity. Combine consommé, water and sherry and pour over goose. Salt and pepper the goose well. Turn goose breast side down on the rack, set in oven and immediately turn down heat to 350°. Roast until tender, about 25 minutes per pound. Baste often or cover the roaster. Serves 6-8.

Zucchini Casserole

½ pound bacon, diced
1 cup onion, chopped
2 pounds zucchini
1 pound sharp cheddar cheese, grated
6 fresh tomatoes, sliced or 2 cups canned tomatoes, sliced
2 cups cracker crumbs
½ teaspoon pepper
1 teaspoon salt

Fry bacon until crisp. Remove with slotted spoon and drain on paper towel. Pour off all but 4 tablespoons fat. Brown onion in bacon fat until golden. Wash zucchini, cut off stems and ends, slice into ¼-inch pieces. In a 2-quart casserole, layer and repeat three times: zucchini, cheese, tomatoes, onions, bacon, cracker crumbs and seasonings. Bake at 350° for 45 minutes. This can be prepared well ahead and baked just before serving. Serves 8.

QUILTING HINT: *Use long strips of masking tape to mark parallel quilting lines. Quilt along the tape's edge, peel it off and move the tape to the next line.*

Double Wedding Ring

Double Wedding Ring is the name usually given to this quilt. Sometimes it is called simply Wedding Ring, but there is at least one other pattern named Wedding Ring, and it looks nothing like this one. Robert Bishop of the Henry Ford Museum has said that this quilt is often poorly executed, but effective when properly drafted and patched. "Effective" would be an understatement for this dinner — when the directions are carefully followed.

MENU
LIMA BEANS ON HAM SLICE

RAW CAULIFLOWER SALAD

BREAD STICKS

PEACHES WITH CHUTNEY

QUILTING HINT: *Be sure to sign and date your quilts. It will add to the enjoyment and value of the quilt in years to come*

Lima Beans on Ham Slice

1 *center cut ham slice, 1 inch thick*
1 *package frozen baby lima beans*
2 *cups grated cheddar cheese*

Broil ham 10 minutes on each side. Prepare lima beans according to package directions. Drain and arrange on top of cooked ham slice. Top with grated cheese. Return to broiler, reduce heat and heat until cheese is melted and slightly browned. Serves 4-6.

Raw Cauliflower Salad

1 *small head cauliflower*
2 *cups shredded lettuce*
½ *cup French dressing*

Separate cauliflower into florets and cut crosswise into thin slices. Mix with lettuce and toss with French dressing. Serves 6.

Peaches with Chutney

Drain 1 can peach halves. Place in a small heat-proof serving dish and top each half with 2 teaspoons chutney. Heat in 350° oven about 10 minutes or until warmed through. Serve warm.

Tulip

Tulip is one of hundreds of appliqué flower patterns, in this case with green stems and leaves and multicolored fabric for the flowers. The rhubarb for this sauce is an early spring vegetable, as the tulip is an early spring flower.

MENU

SWEET-SOUR BEEF BALLS WITH PINEAPPLE AND PEPPERS

RICE

RHUBARB SAUCE AND COOKIES

Sweet-Sour Beef Balls with Pineapple and Peppers

1 *pound ground beef*
1 *egg*
1 *tablespoon cornstarch*
½ *teaspoon salt*
2 *tablespoons chopped onion*
3 *tablespoons cooking oil*
1 *cup pineapple juice*
3 *tablespoons cornstarch*
1 *tablespoon soy sauce*
3 *tablespoons vinegar*
6 *tablespoons water*
½ *cup sugar*
4 *slices canned pineapple, cut in pieces*
2 *green peppers, cut in thin strips*

Mix together beef, egg, cornstarch, salt and chopped onion. Form into 18 balls and brown in hot oil. Drain. Heat pineapple juice in pan over low heat for a few minutes. Combine cornstarch, soy sauce, vinegar, water and sugar, add to pan and cook sauce until thick, stirring constantly. Place meat balls, pineapple pieces and green pepper strips in sauce and heat thoroughly. Serve over rice. Serves 6.

Rhubarb Sauce

2 *pounds rhubarb*
½ *cup hot water*
¾ *cup sugar*
Cinnamon

Cut off leaves and stem ends of rhubarb, wash and cut into 1-inch pieces. In a saucepan, place rhubarb and hot water, cover, and simmer for 10 minutes. Add sugar and simmer 5 minutes more. Spoon into small dessert dishes and top with a dash of cinnamon. Serves 6.

COOKING HINT: *One pound of raw rhubarb will make three half-cup servings when cooked.*

Wheel of Fortune

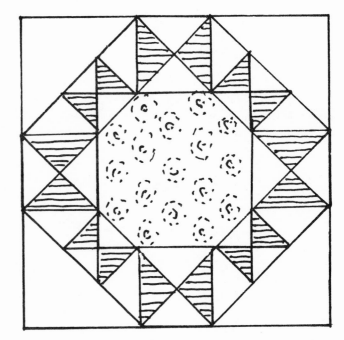

Wheel of Fortune is one of at least five patterns with this name — and, as is usual, each of the patterns has other names too. The "wheel of fortune" in this menu is made of spinach and, with the pork and sweet potatoes, will make any family think the cook is worth a fortune to them.

MENU
ROAST PORK

SPINACH RING

BAKED SWEET POTATOES

ICE CREAM AND WAFER COOKIES

Roast Pork

1 4-pound pork loin roast, bone in
Salt and pepper to taste

Preheat oven to 350°. Rub roast with salt and pepper and place, fat side up, in an open roaster. Roast about 2½ hours or until meat thermometer reaches 185°. Serves 6.

Spinach Ring

1 tablespoon butter
1 tablespoon flour
½ cup whole milk or light cream
3 eggs, separated
2 packages frozen chopped spinach, thawed and drained
Salt and pepper to taste
Tiny cooked onions, leftover sliced vegetables or
    black olives

In a saucepan over medium heat, melt butter, add flour and stir until well blended. Remove from heat and add milk, stirring constantly. Return to heat, continue stirring and cook until sauce is thick. Remove from heat. Beat egg yolks lightly; beat in small amount of hot sauce, then add yolks gradually to saucepan. Stir in spinach. Fold in stiffly beaten egg whites, salt and pepper. Pour mixture into a well-greased ring mold. Cover mold with foil, set in a pan of hot water and bake at 350° for 30 to 40 minutes. Invert on a serving platter and fill the center with tiny cooked onions, leftover sliced vegetables or black olives. Serves 6.

Baked Sweet Potatoes

Select 6 medium-sized sweet potatoes. Wash well and pierce with a fork. Bake at 350° for 45 to 60 minutes or until soft to the touch.

QUILTING HINT: Unless the quilt has curved or circular edges, there is no reason to cut the binding strips on the bias. Long straight strips do the job well.

Rolling Stone

This pattern, Rolling Stone, looks much like a stone heading rapidly down the hill, gathering no moss. The speedy hash won't gather moss either, but it will garner praise.

MENU

SPEEDY CORNED BEEF HASH

TWO-BEAN SALAD

BROWNIES

Speedy Corned Beef Hash

1 can corned beef hash
1 onion, diced
½ cup ketchup
1 egg, slightly beaten
1 tablespoon Worcestershire sauce
2 tablespoons butter or margarine

Combine hash with onion, ketchup, egg and Worcestershire sauce. Melt butter in a skillet, press hash evenly into pan and fry until brown and heated through. Top with poached eggs if desired. Serves 4-6.

Two-Bean Salad

Make the night before or early in the day.

1 16-ounce can garbanzo beans, drained
1 15½-ounce can red kidney beans, drained
1 8-ounce can tomato sauce
¼ cup salad oil
¼ cup wine vinegar
3 tablespoons chopped onion
½ cup chopped celery
Salad greens

Combine all ingredients except salad greens. Cover and refrigerate overnight or all day. To serve, drain and spoon onto salad greens. Serves 8.

Brownies

1 cup sugar
½ cup butter
2 squares unsweetened chocolate
2 eggs, lightly beaten
1 teaspoon salt
½ cup flour
1 teaspoon vanilla
1 cup chopped walnuts

In a saucepan, melt sugar, butter and chocolate. Add eggs, salt, flour, vanilla and nuts. Mix well and pour into a greased baking pan. Bake at 350° for 20 minutes. When cool, cut into squares.

COOKING HINT: *Three tablespoons of cocoa plus one tablespoon of fat may be used to substitute for one square of unsweetened chocolate.*

Jack-in-the-Box

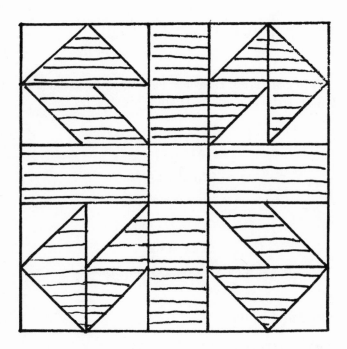

This Jack-in-the-Box pattern must have reminded its maker of the exploded jack-in-the-box that her child was playing with. Jack would have left Jill, or Mr. Sprat his wife, at the mere thought of a meal like this one.

MENU
VERMICELLI WITH TOMATO AND SEAFOOD

GREEN BEANS

FRENCH BREAD

FRESH PEARS AND BLEU CHEESE

Vermicelli with Tomato and Seafood

1 onion, minced
2 cloves garlic, minced
2 tablespoons olive oil
1 16-ounce can tomatoes
¼ teaspoon sugar
½ teaspoon dried basil
½ teaspoon salt
Dash of pepper
⅓ cup sherry or white wine
1 4- or 6-ounce can shrimp or crabmeat
8 ounces vermicelli

Cook onion and garlic in olive oil until soft. Add tomatoes, sugar, basil, salt and pepper. Simmer for 30 minutes or until slightly reduced. Add sherry or white wine and seafood and heat to simmering; do not boil. Cook vermicelli according to package directions. Drain well. Serve sauce over hot pasta. Serves 4.

Green Beans

If using fresh green beans, snap off top and bottom tips. Slice diagonally and cook in a minimum of water until slightly crunchy, about 15 minutes. Season with salt and pepper and a pat of butter. For frozen beans, follow package directions.

QUILTING HINT: Quilting patterns with long straight lines can be marked with the aid of a yardstick.

Twist and Turn

Twist and Turn is made from three fabrics for its braided, twisted effect. For a new twist, turn to this skewered lamb.

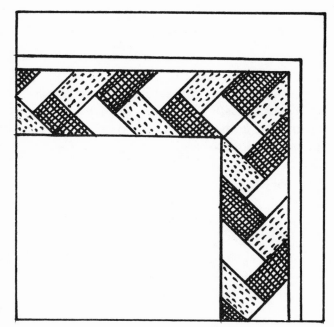

MENU
SKEWERED LAMB

MASHED POTATOES

SPICY GOLDEN CARROTS

COLE SLAW

CHOCOLATE-APRICOT PUDDING

Skewered Lamb

2 pounds boneless lamb from leg or loin
Salt and pepper
Bacon slices
½ cup melted butter
½ cup fine bread crumbs

Cut lamb in 1-inch cubes, season with salt and pepper. Thread lamb on skewers with 1-inch pieces of bacon between cubes. Brush with melted butter, then roll in bread crumbs. Broil in oven or over charcoal, turning often until evenly browned on all sides. Serves 6.

Spicy Golden Carrots

Scrape 6 to 8 fresh carrots and cut in thick diagonal slices. Cover with water and add 3 whole cloves. Cook until barely tender, about 15 minutes. Drain and serve hot. Serves 6.

Cole Slaw

¼ cup mayonnaise
¼ cup corn syrup
1 tablespoon lemon juice
Salt to taste
½ teaspoon celery seed
1 tablespoon finely minced onion or green onion
1 small head cabbage, shredded

Put all ingredients except cabbage in a bowl and mix together well. Add cabbage and toss. Serve chilled. Serves 6.

Chocolate-Apricot Pudding

½ cup butter
1½ cups flour
1 egg
2 tablespoons cream
¾ cup dried apricots
1½ cups sugar
7 eggs, separated
3 ounces bitter chocolate
4 ounces sweet chocolate

Cut butter into flour until fine; mix in egg beaten with cream. Press a thin layer of dough in the bottom of a 10-inch pie plate. Bake at 375° until lightly tan, about 5 to 6 minutes. Meanwhile, simmer apricots in water to cover, with ½ cup sugar until soft, 15 to 20 minutes. Beat egg yolks with remaining sugar. Melt chocolate with a little water and cool. Combine chocolate with egg yolks and fold in stiffly beaten egg whites. Arrange apricots in crust, pour in chocolate mixture and bake at 400° for 20 minutes. Cool before serving. Serves 8.

COOKING HINT: *Set the table early; then, even if the meal is delayed, it'll appear as if food is imminent. This may placate the hungry grouches in the other room.*

Hexagon

Hexagon, sometimes called Ferris Wheel, was originally copied from the design on the cover of a kitchen table — or so the story goes. Perhaps it could also be called Ring Mold, after the beet and horseradish ring in this menu.

MENU

BAKED CHICKEN SANDWICH

BEET AND HORSERADISH RING

SLICED BANANAS AND CREAM

Baked Chicken Sandwich

These sandwiches can be made ahead and kept frozen.

16 *slices white bread*
1½ *cup diced, cooked chicken*
1 *10¾-ounce can mushroom soup*
½ *10½-ounce can chicken gravy*
2 *tablespoons minced pimiento*
2 *tablespoons minced green onion*
1 *5-ounce can water chestnuts, chopped*
4 *eggs*
2 *tablespoons milk*
1 *6½-ounce bag potato chips, crushed*

Trim crusts from bread. Combine next 6 ingredients and spoon mixture onto 8 slices of bread. Close sandwiches, wrap tightly in foil and freeze. When ready to serve, beat eggs with milk; dip frozen sandwiches in egg, then in crushed potato chips. Place on a greased jelly-roll pan and bake at 300° for 1 hour. Serves 8.

Beet and Horseradish Ring

1 *package lemon gelatin*
2 *cups boiling water or beet juice*
Juice of 1 lemon
1 *1-pound can beets, drained and chopped fine*
¼ *teaspoon salt*
4 *tablespoons prepared horseradish*
Russian dressing

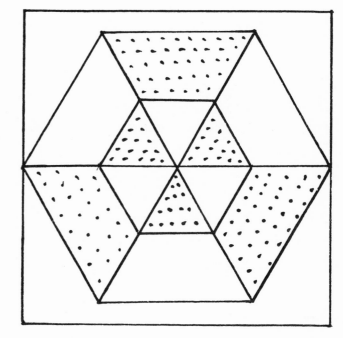

Dissolve gelatin in boiling water or beet juice. Add lemon juice. Chill until partially set. Add beets, salt and horseradish. Pour into an oiled ring mold and chill until firm, about 3 to 4 hours. Invert on a bed of shredded lettuce and serve with dressing in a bowl in the center of the ring. Serves 8.

QUILTING HINT: *If machine piecing, set machine for 12 stitches per inch.*

Tic Tac Toe

Tic Tac Toe is an old pattern, also known as Kitty Corner and Puss-in-boots. You could play tic tac toe on these delectable buttermilk waffles, but you'd probably rather fill their squares with maple syrup.

MENU

WAFFLES WITH MAPLE SYRUP

BACON, CANADIAN BACON OR HAM SLICES

HOT FRUIT DESSERT

Waffles

2 eggs
2 cups buttermilk
2 cups flour
2 teaspoons baking powder
1 teaspoon baking soda
½ teaspoon salt
¼ cup plus 2 tablespoons cooking oil
Chopped nuts

In a blender or by hand, mix all ingredients until smooth, about 2 minutes. Bake in a waffle iron. Serve sprinkled with chopped nuts. Makes 6-8 waffles.

Hot Fruit Dessert

1 8-ounce can peach halves, drained
1 8-ounce can apricot halves, drained
1 8-ounce can pitted black cherries, drained
¼ cup orange juice
¼ cup lemon juice
1 teaspoon orange rind, grated
1 teaspoon lemon rind, grated
4 tablespoons brown sugar

Place fruit in ovenproof dish. Combine all other ingredients, bring to boil and pour over fruit. Heat about 15 minutes at 350°. Serve plain or, for a special touch, with a dash of whipped cream or sour cream on top. Serves 6.

COOKING HINT: Save the fat after cooking bacon, refrigerated, to use in other cooking. It adds seasoning and flavor besides being economical.

Irish Puzzle

Irish Puzzle is a most popular quilt. This is proven by the number of names given to the pattern: Forest Path, Rambling Road, Climbing Rose, Storm at Sea, North Wind, Tangled Tares, Indian Trail, Winding Walk, Rambling Rose, Old Maid's Ramble, Flying Dutchman, Weather Vane. We like ''Irish Puzzle'' — and this Irish Coffee.

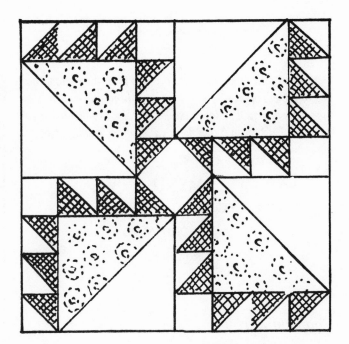

MENU
CHICKEN JUBILEE

BUTTERED BROWN RICE

GREEN BEANS WITH ONION-FLAVORED ALMONDS

IRISH COFFEE

HOT CHOCOLATE

Chicken Jubilee

6 chicken breasts or 8 chicken thighs
Lemon juice
Seasoned flour
½ cup margarine
½ can cream of mushroom soup
½ soup can sour cream
1 21-ounce can pitted Bing cherries
Parsley sprigs

Marinate chicken in lemon juice for an hour or so. Drain off juice and lightly dust chicken with seasoned flour. In 350° oven, melt margarine in an ovenproof dish. Place chicken in dish and bake, uncovered, for 45 minutes. Mix mushroom soup and sour cream and pour over chicken; bake 15 minutes longer. In a saucepan, heat cherries. Just before serving, lift cherries from juice with a slotted spoon and arrange around chicken. Garnish with parsley sprigs. Serves 4-6.

Green Beans with Onion-flavored Almonds

Cook beans in boiling salted water until just tender. Dress with butter, salt and pepper. Sprinkle with onion-flavored toasted almond slivers.

Irish Coffee

Sugar
Hot, strong coffee
Irish whiskey
Whipped cream

In a glass cup or stemmed goblet, place 1 teaspoon granulated sugar. Fill glass ¾ full of hot coffee. Stir to dissolve sugar. Add 1 ounce whiskey and stir once. Carefully float 1 tablespoon whipped cream on top of coffee. Makes 1 serving.

COOKING HINT: A good, speedy hot chocolate mix: one cup each of granulated sugar and dry milk and ¾ cup of unsweetened cocoa, sifted together and kept in a covered jar. Use 4 to 6 heaping teaspoons to a mug. Fill the mug with boiling water and stir; top with a marshmallow.

Arabic Lattice

Arabic Lattice may have been copied from the design on a tile, or a piece of printed fabric, for such things have often been the source of a quilt design. Eggplant Arabic has the aromas of the Near East, even if you don't eat it under a silken tent.

COOKING HINT: *Macaroni doubles in volume when cooked; noodles increase by a third.*

MENU
EGGPLANT ARABIC

MACARONI SALAD

CRUSTY ROLLS

CHILLED GRAPES

Eggplant Arabic

1 medium eggplant
1 cup cottage cheese
1 egg
¼ teaspoon salt
1 slice bread, crumbled
½ teaspoon basil
½ teaspoon oregano
¼ cup snipped fresh parsley
2 8-ounce cans tomato sauce
Parmesan cheese
2 teaspoons margarine

Wash and slice eggplant into ½-inch slices. In a mixing bowl, combine cottage cheese, egg, salt, bread, basil, oregano and parsley. Pour ¼ cup tomato sauce into bottom of a 8-by-12-inch baking dish. Place a layer of eggplant in dish; pour over half of the remaining tomato sauce. Spread with cottage cheese mixture. Add another layer of eggplant and rest of tomato sauce. Sprinkle top with Parmesan cheese, dot with margarine, cover with foil and bake at 350° for 45 minutes. Serves 4-6.

Macaroni Salad

3 cups salad macaroni
½ cup sandwich spread
½ cup creamy French dressing

Cook macaroni according to package directions. Drain and cool. Mix well with sandwich spread and French dressing. Chill until served. Serves 6.

Kansas Troubles

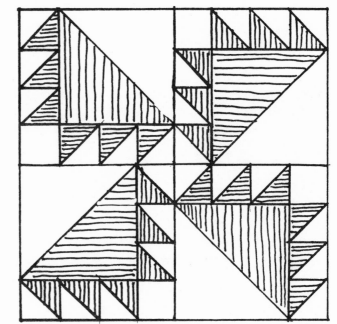

"Kansas Troubles" was a phrase with political connotations from 1840 to 1861, during the political wrangling over where slavery would be legal. If there's been trouble convincing your family that liver is delicious, perhaps this sautéed liver will be a solution.

MENU
SAUTÉED LIVER

PEAS WITH MINT

DUTCH ONION RINGS

DATE STICKS

Sautéed Liver

1 pound beef liver cut into 1-inch cubes
Milk to cover
¼ cup flour
½ teaspoon salt
Dash of pepper
2 cloves garlic, minced
¼ cup margarine

Soak liver in milk for ½ hour to remove strong taste. Drain thoroughly. Toss in flour seasoned with salt and pepper. Cook with garlic in margarine until lightly browned but still pink inside. Serves 4.

Peas with Mint

1 package frozen peas
4-5 fresh mint leaves or ½ teaspoon dried mint
Margarine

Cook frozen peas following package directions. Sprinkle dry or fresh chopped mint over cooked peas. Add margarine and toss. Serves 4.

Dutch Onion Rings

2 medium onions
¼ cup sour cream
¼ teaspoon salt
½ teaspoon celery seed
1 teaspoon lemon juice

Slice onions ¼ inch thick and separate into rings. Place in bowl and cover with boiling water. Let stand 2 minutes. Drain and chill. Mix sour cream, salt, celery seed and lemon juice. Toss with onions just before serving. Serves 4.

Date Sticks

1 cup flour
1 teaspoon baking powder
½ teaspoon salt
1 cup sugar
2 eggs
1 tablespoon melted margarine or cooking oil
2 cups chopped dates
½ cup chopped nuts
3 tablespoons hot water

Sift together flour, baking powder and salt. Beat sugar and eggs together. Add margarine and stir in dates and nuts. Add dry ingredients alternately with hot water, beating well after each addition. Divide mixture into 2 greased 8-inch square pans (freeze one panful for later), spreading the dough thin. Bake at 325° for 30-35 minutes. Cool and cut in 1-inch-by-4-inch strips. Remove from pan and roll in powdered sugar. Whole recipe makes 2⅔ dozen.

QUILTING HINT: *Velcro strips, one half sewn to the quilt, the other half glued to a strip of wood, make quilts used as wall hangings easy to install.*

Village Church

Village Church is one of many patterns that show buildings in everyday life in early America; there were dozens of school houses and barns, too. For Sunday dinner, after church, what could be better than this meat casserole, made ahead to lessen the Sabbath work?

MENU

HEARTY MEAT CASSEROLE

TOSSED GREENS WITH ONION RINGS

BUTTERED FRENCH LOAVES

FRESH FRUIT WITH CHEESE

Hearty Meat Casserole

This can be prepared several days in advance and stored in the refrigerator.

2 pounds ground beef
2 large onions, chopped
1 green pepper, chopped
Olive oil
1 12-ounce package flat egg noodles
2 12-ounce cans whole corn, drained
1 20-ounce can tomatoes
2 10½-ounce cans tamales, sliced in ½-inch rings
1 7¾-ounce can pitted ripe olives
1 4-ounce can mushroom stems and pieces
1 teaspoon chili powder
½ teaspoon curry powder (optional)
1 cup sharp cheese, grated

Heat oil and brown beef, onions and pepper together. Boil noodles in salted water according to package directions; drain well. Place noodles in a large, oiled baking dish. Add meat mixture, corn, tomatoes, tamales, olives and mushrooms and mix gently. Season to taste with chili powder and curry powder. Sprinkle cheese over top and bake at 350° for 45 minutes or until heated through. Serves 10-12.

Tossed Greens with Onion Rings

2-3 heads lettuce
2 large Bermuda onions, sliced
French dressing

Wash and dry lettuce. Tear greens into bite-sized pieces and put in a large salad bowl. Separate onion slices into rings and add to greens. Toss with your favorite French dressing. Serves 10-12.

Fresh Fruit with Cheese

As a table centerpiece, arrange a large platter of fresh fruit such as whole pears, peaches, plums, grapes, pineapple. At dessert time, bring out 2 or 3 types of cheese on cutting boards with knives.

QUILTING HINT: To avoid having to quilt through several thicknesses, put quilting stitches at least a quarter-inch from the seam line. (This assumes you've used quarter-inch seam allowances.)

Buttercup

Gilbert and Sullivan's unforgettable character was called Little Buttercup, though she could never tell why. It's easy to tell why this pattern was so named; it will almost reflect yellow under an admirer's chin. Butterscotch pudding will bring reminders of another Gilbert and Sullivan character when your audience starts saying, "Yum yum."

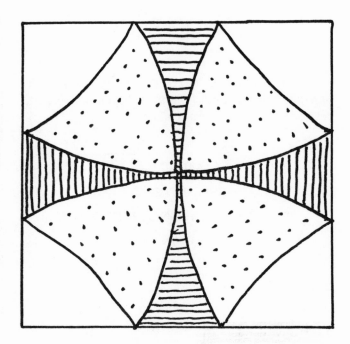

MENU
CHILI AND CHEESE QUICHE

SALAD JULIENNE

BUTTERSCOTCH PUDDING

Chili and Cheese Quiche

1 9-inch pie shell (frozen or homemade)
1 cup frozen corn, thawed
1 4-ounce can diced green chiles
1½ cups shredded cheddar cheese
1 cup chopped onion
3 eggs, slightly beaten
½ cup half and half
2 tablespoons sour cream
¼ teaspoon salt
¼ teaspoon pepper

Partially bake pie shell for 8 minutes at 400°. (If using frozen shell, follow directions on wrapper.) Layer corn, chiles, cheese and onion in pie shell. In a bowl, stir together eggs, half and half, sour cream, salt and pepper. Pour egg mixture over vegetables. Bake at 375° for 35 to 45 minutes or until knife inserted halfway between edge and center of quiche comes out clean. Let stand 5 minutes before serving. Serves 4-6.

Salad Julienne

1 cup raw carrots, julienned
1 cup canned green beans, French style
1 cup cooked or raw peas
½ cup French dressing
Watercress or shredded lettuce

Put vegetables in a salad bowl. Add dressing, cover and marinate in refrigerator for 30 minutes before serving. Add greens, toss lightly and serve. Serves 4-6.

Butterscotch Pudding

⅔ cup brown sugar, packed
2 tablespoons cornstarch
⅛ teaspoon salt
3 cups milk
2 eggs, separated
2 tablespoons margarine
1 teaspoon vanilla
2 tablespoons sugar

In top of a double boiler mix brown sugar, cornstarch and salt. Add milk gradually to sugar mixture. Stir constantly over medium heat until pudding thickens. Cook in double boiler 20 minutes. Lightly mix egg yolks and add several spoons of hot pudding to them, then add to rest of pudding, stirring constantly. Cook for several more minutes. Remove from heat and add margarine and vanilla. Cool. Meanwhile, beat egg whites with sugar until stiff. Fold gently into cooled pudding. Chill until serving time. Serves 4-6.

COOKING HINT: Directions calling for "brown sugar packed" mean exactly that. When properly packed, the sugar should retain the shape of the cup when it's turned out.

X-quisite

X-quisite is an effective over-all design, deceptively simple. Sherried Crab and Artichokes with Herb Sauce are simple to put together — and are also exquisite.

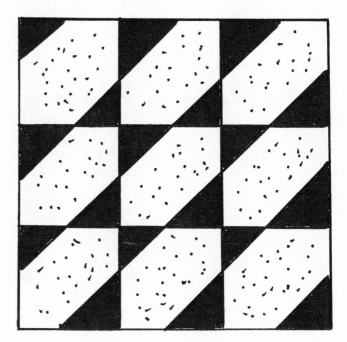

MENU

SHERRIED CRAB

ARTICHOKES WITH VINAIGRETTE SAUCE

FLAN

Sherried Crab

3 tablespoons butter
3 tablespoons flour
2 cups milk
2 tablespoons sherry
1 pound crab meat
1 package frozen patty shells
Paprika

Melt butter and stir in flour until well blended. Remove from heat and gradually add milk. Return to heat and cook until thick, stirring constantly. Stir in sherry, add crab meat and heat through. Bake patty shells according to package directions. Fill patty shells with hot crab mixture and sprinkle with paprika. Serves 6.

Artichokes with Vinaigrette Sauce

6 artichokes
6 tablespoons oil
2 tablespoons wine vinegar
½ teaspoon each salt and dill weed
1 teaspoon snipped parsley
Dash of dried savory

Wash artichokes and cut off stems at the base. Stand artichokes in a deep saucepan and add about 3 inches of water. Cover and boil gently 35 to 45 minutes or until base can be pierced easily with a fork. Lift from pot and drain.

When cool, gently spread leaves and remove choke from center. Combine oil and vinegar with seasonings and chill. Serve as a dip with artichokes. Serves 6.

Flan

¾ cup sugar, divided
2 eggs
1 13-ounce can evaporated milk
1 teaspoon vanilla
⅛ teaspoon salt

Stir ½ cup sugar in heavy frying pan until it melts and becomes light brown. Pour into a mold, tilting to coat the sides. Beat eggs in a bowl; add milk, remaining sugar, vanilla and salt. Stir to blend and pour into mold. Set mold in a pan of hot water 1 inch deep. Bake at 325° for 50 minutes. Chill. Serves 4-6.

COOKING HINT: *Press large slices of bread, with crusts removed, into muffin pans and brown in the oven for patty shells.*

72

Bleeding Heart

Bleeding Heart was not so named because its designer suffered a broken romance but because it is one of many flower patterns — in this case a pink member of the poppy family with drooping heart-shaped blossoms. The quilter who serves this meal isn't likely to have a broken heart either — at least not as a result of her cooking.

MENU

SHIRRED EGGS IN TOMATOES

ROLLED HAM SLICES

ENGLISH MUFFIN BITS

ASSORTED FRESH FRUIT

Shirred Eggs in Tomatoes

Allow 1 medium-sized tomato per person.

Cut thin slice from stem end of tomato and scoop out pulp and seeds. Salt inside of tomato. Break one egg and slide into tomato. Sprinkle with salt and pepper and cover with buttered bread crumbs. Bake at 350° until delicately browned and egg is set, about 10 minutes or less. Serves 1.

Rolled Ham Slices

3 ounces cream cheese
¼ cup chopped nuts or chopped olives
2 or 3 thin slices boiled or baked ham per person

Soften cream cheese, mix with nuts or olives and spread on ham slices. Roll slices. Heat if desired, or serve cold.

English Muffin Bits

Allow 1 English muffin per person.

Toast and butter muffins, spread with a variety of jams and cut into quarters. Serve hot.

QUILTING HINT: Decorating a birthday cake for a quilter? Make a frosting quilt block on top of the cake.

Interacting Pyramids

Interacting Pyramids is a dazzling design that may make you think the beer stew has affected your vision. Not so — the alcohol cooks away, and those circles are red apples and walnuts.

MENU
BEER STEW

QUICK ZUCCHINI

MINIATURE DILL LOAVES

CHILLED RED APPLES, WALNUT MEATS
AND CHEESE

Beer Stew

1 *clove garlic, minced*
2 *tablespoons oil*
2 *pounds lean stewing beef, cut in 1-inch cubes*
1 *teaspoon salt*
2 *large onions, sliced*
1 *can beer*
1 *tomato, sliced*
1 *bay leaf*
¼ *teaspoon thyme*
2 *teaspoons Worcestershire sauce*
⅛ *teaspoon cayenne*
Instant potato

In a skillet, sauté garlic in hot oil until golden. Add meat and brown slowly on all sides. Sprinkle with salt. Transfer meat to an ovenproof casserole. Sauté onions in the skillet until transparent, adding a little more oil if necessary. Arrange onions over meat in casserole. Pour beer into skillet; add tomato, bay leaf, thyme, Worcestershire sauce and cayenne. Bring to boil and pour over meat. Cook, covered, at 275° for 4 hours. When ready to serve, sprinkle with instant potato — just enough to thicken the gravy. Serves 4-6.

Quick Zucchini

4-6 *medium zucchini*
1 *tablespoon margarine*
Salt and pepper

Wash zucchini, cut off stem ends and grate coarsely. Melt margarine in skillet. Add grated zucchini and toss until well coated with margarine. Season with salt and pepper. Cover pan, turn off heat. Serve in 3 to 5 minutes. Serves 4.

Miniature Dill Loaves

1 *package refrigerator baking-powder biscuits*
4 *tablespoons margarine, melted*
½ *teaspoon dried dill weed*

Separate 12 biscuits. Roll in melted margarine so all sides are coated. Stand 4 biscuits sideways in each of 3 ungreased individual loaf pans. Sprinkle with dill weed. Place pans on cookie sheet for easy handling. Bake at 375° for 10-13 minutes. (Individual loaf pans can be made from double-thick aluminum foil folded to 4 by 2½ by 1½ inches.) Makes 3 loaves.

Chilled Red Apples, Walnut Meats and Cheese

In a shallow serving dish, make a pretty arrangement of shelled walnut meats, wedges of red apples and a red-coated Edam cheese cut in sections.

COOKING HINT: *Instant potato makes a great thickening for stews and gravies — it doesn't lump.*

Strawberry

Strawberry is a pattern not easily visualized at first — but if you use the right colors and squint through half-closed eyes, you can see the berry and even the green sepals beneath. Strawberry fluff is a pleasant, light ending to this hearty meal.

MENU

GAZPACHO (COLD SPANISH SOUP)

HEARTY FRIED RICE

STRAWBERRY FLUFF

Gazpacho

1 1-pound can tomatoes, undrained
1 clove garlic
½ teaspoon salt
¼ teaspoon pepper
1 small onion, chopped
½ green pepper, chopped
½ cucumber, peeled and seeded
1 stalk celery, chopped
2 tablespoons wine vinegar
3 tablespoons cooking oil
½ cup water
Dash of Worcestershire sauce
⅛ teaspoon cayenne

Put all ingredients in blender and buzz for 30 seconds. Chill before serving. Serves 4-6.

Hearty Fried Rice

2 tablespoons oil
½ cup onions, chopped
2 cups cold, cooked rice
2 eggs
1 tablespoon soy sauce
¼ teaspoon salt
2 cups leftover ham, pork, or cooked shrimp

Fry onions in oil until lightly brown. Add cooked rice and sauté. Beat eggs slightly with soy sauce and salt; stir into rice and sauté until hot and eggs are cooked to your liking. This dish may be varied according to the contents of your refrigerator; you may add chopped green pepper, sliced water chestnuts, sliced mushrooms or chopped peanuts for variety. Heat through. Serves 4-6.

Strawberry Fluff

1 cup fresh sliced strawberries
1 teaspoon lemon juice
1 egg white (at room temperature)
¾ cup sugar

Put all ingredients in small bowl or electric mixer. Beat until mixture forms stiff peaks. Refrigerate until ready to serve. Serves 6.

COOKING HINT: Cook some extra rice and save to make fried rice.

Buck and Wing

The Buck and Wing was a dance that seems to have disappeared with vaudeville. The Cornish language became extinct in the eighteenth century, but the Cornish hen has survived as the descendant of a superb fowl for the table.

MENU

ROCK CORNISH HENS

ZUCCHINI WITH WALNUTS

ROMAINE AND MUSHROOM SALAD

MELON RINGS WITH SHERBET OR ICE CREAM

Rock Cornish Hens

4 1-pound frozen rock Cornish hens, thawed
Salt and pepper
4 teaspoons dried thyme
½ cup butter, melted
2 tablespoons lemon juice
Dash paprika

Preheat oven to 400°. Sprinkle salt, pepper and thyme inside each hen. Make a basting sauce of butter, lemon juice and paprika. Arrange hens in a large roasting pan. Roast, basting several times, for 1 hour or until browned and tender. Serves 4.

Zucchini with Walnuts

3 tablespoons butter, divided
½ cup coarsely chopped walnuts
1½ pounds zucchini
2 tablespoons butter
½ teaspoon salt
Pepper

Heat 1 tablespoon butter in a small skillet, add walnuts and toss until lightly browned. Set aside. Wash zucchini and cut into ½-inch slices. Sauté zucchini in 2 tablespoons butter just until soft, about 3 to 5 minutes. Add walnuts, salt and pepper and serve hot. Serves 4-6.

Romaine and Mushroom Salad

1 head romaine
¼ pound fresh mushrooms, sliced
Vinaigrette dressing

Wash lettuce and dry well. Tear into bite-sized pieces and put in a salad bowl. Add sliced mushrooms, toss with dressing and serve at once. Serves 4.

Melon Rings with Sherbet or Ice Cream

Cut a chilled cantaloupe, honeydew or casaba into rings. Discard seeds and fill hollows with lemon or lime sherbet or vanilla ice cream.

QUILTING HINT: When joining two seamed patches, make sure the unopened seams are pressed in opposite directions so the bulk will be distributed.

Star Light

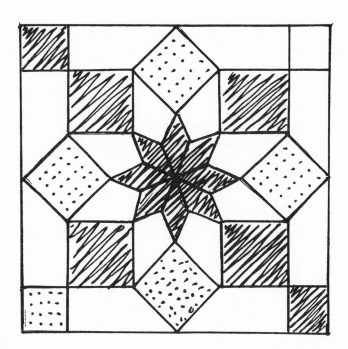

"Star light, star bright" was the beginning of many a wish when the first star winked in the evening sky. If you wish for a memorable meal of lobster and an unusual chocolate pie, here is your wish come true.

MENU

LOBSTER NEWBURG

REFRIGERATOR MASHED POTATOES

TOMATO ASPIC

FRENCH SILK CHOCOLATE PIE

Lobster Newburg

2 *cups lobster meat*
1 *tablespoon butter*
1 *cup cream*
3 *egg yolks, beaten*
¼ *cup sherry*

Sauté lobster in butter. Add cream and bring to a boil. Warm egg yolks with ¼ cup hot cream, then pour into cream. Add sherry and cook 3 minutes or until slightly thickened. Serve in a ring of mashed potatoes. Serves 6-8.

Refrigerator Mashed Potatoes

5 *pounds potatoes*
2 *3-ounce packages cream cheese*
1 *cup sour cream*
2 *teaspoons onion salt*
1 *teaspoon salt*
¼ *teaspoon pepper*
2 *tablespoons butter*

Peel, cook and mash potatoes. Add other ingredients and beat until smooth, light and fluffy. Cool, cover and keep in refrigerator for as long as two weeks. To use: spoon desired amount into buttered casserole, dot with butter and bake uncovered at 350° for 30 minutes. For the Newburg, make a ring of the potatoes in a casserole, bake as directed. Just before serving, pile Newburg in center of ring. Serves 6-8.

French Silk Chocolate Pie

1½ *sticks butter*
¾ *cup sugar*
1½ *ounces bitter chocolate, melted*
1 *teaspoon vanilla*
2 *eggs*
1 *8-inch baked pie shell*
Whipped cream

With an electric mixer, cream butter; gradually cream in sugar. Blend in cooled chocolate and vanilla. Add eggs one at a time, beating 4 to 5 minutes after each. Pour into pie shell and chill several hours or overnight. Serve with whipped cream. Serves 6-8.

QUILTING HINT: *It is tempting to use pretty sheets for quilt backings. However, the blends and tightly woven percales are hard to quilt.*

Roman Stripe

Roman Stripe is a refined and disciplined version of the crazy quilt. Although this elegant stew was named after Count Paul Stroganoff, it probably had no more connection with Russia than the quilt pattern had with ancient Italy.

MENU
BEEF STROGANOFF

BUTTERED NOODLES

EGGPLANT PROVENÇAL

FRESH FRUITS OF THE SEASON

Beef Stroganoff

Less tender cuts of beef may be used, since this dish simmers for two hours.

1½ pounds beef, cut in finger-sized pieces
Seasoned flour
3 tablespoons margarine
2 medium onions, sliced
2 cloves garlic, minced
1 teaspoon Worcestershire sauce
2 tablespoons ketchup
½ cup water
1 4-ounce can button mushrooms
¾ cup sour cream

Flour the meat in a mixture of ¼ cup flour, 1 teaspoon salt and ¼ teaspoon pepper. Melt margarine in heavy skillet. Add meat in small batches, browning on all sides. Do not crowd the meat or it will steam rather than brown. Add onions and garlic and cook over medium heat until onions are lightly golden. Return meat to skillet and add Worcestershire sauce, ketchup, water and liquid from canned mushrooms. Cover and simmer (liquid should not boil, but merely quiver) until meat is completely tender, about 2 hours. Five minutes before serving, stir in mushrooms and sour cream. Serve with noodles, prepared according to package directions. Serves 4-6.

Eggplant Provençale

1 eggplant
2 cups fresh tomatoes, seeded and chopped
1 cup chopped onion
1 clove garlic, minced
Pinch of thyme
4 tablespoons chopped parsley
Salt and pepper
Parmesan cheese

Peel eggplant and slice into ½-inch thick slices. Place slices on a lightly oiled cooky sheet and broil about 5 minutes. Set aside. Sauté tomatoes, onions, garlic, thyme and parsley until thickened. Season with salt and pepper. Pile on top of eggplant slices. Sprinkle with cheese and bake at 350° until hot and lightly browned. Serves 4-6.

QUILTING HINT: *To avoid problems of stretching patches with long edges cut on the bias, try cutting the long sides on the straight grain of the cloth. The two shorter sides on the bias can more easily be contained. Or stay-stitch the long biases.*

Love Apple

The love apple was the tomato — thought to be poisonous by the colonists. We have learned that they are delicious and nutritious, and have included a pint of cherry tomatoes in this salad.

MENU

BEEF NOODLE CASSEROLE

VEGETABLE PLATE WITH
OIL AND LEMON DRESSING

HOT CLOVERLEAF ROLLS

FRUIT COMPOTE

Beef Noodle Casserole

This dish is a great way to use leftover roast beef.

4 cups fine noodles
3 cups cooked beef, cut in 1-inch cubes
1 cup beef stock or bouillon
1 onion, chopped
1 cup sliced almonds, toasted
½ pint sour cream
¼ cup milk
¼ teaspoon salt
Pepper and paprika to taste
Soft bread crumbs

Cook noodles according to package directions. Combine all other ingredients and mix with noodles. Place in a buttered casserole and top with bread crumbs. Bake at 350° for 45 minutes. Serves 8.

Vegetable Plate with Oil and Lemon Dressing

1 small head cauliflower
Asparagus tips, cooked or raw
1 pint cherry tomatoes
Lettuce

Separate cauliflower into florets and cook in boiling salted water about 5 minutes. Drain and chill. On lettuce leaves, arrange cauliflower surrounded with asparagus and tomatoes. Serve with dressing. Serves 8.

Oil and Lemon Dressing

3 tablespoons oil
1 tablespoon fresh lemon juice
¼ teaspoon dry mustard
1 small clove garlic, minced
Dash of salt and pepper

Mix ingredients together until smooth. Chill until ready to serve. Makes ½ cup.

Fruit Compote

1 can Kadota figs, drained
2 oranges, peeled and sectioned
1 apple, cored and diced
Sherry
Nutmeg

Combine figs, oranges and apple in a bowl and chill until dessert time. Top each serving with a tablespoon of sherry and a dash of nutmeg.

QUILTING HINT: Gift-wrap paper and greeting cards may have usable design ideas for original quilt block patterns. The illustrations in children's books are also a good source of designs, especially for appliqué.

Cat and Mice

Cat and Mice is one of several patterns with that name — perhaps indicating that mice, and therefore cats, were familiar to the early quilters. Besides mice, cats love liver, and their owners will relish this liver flavored with sesame.

MENU

SESAME LIVER

OVEN-BROWNED POTATOES

ZUCCHINI WITH TOMATOES

ORANGE CAKE

Sesame Liver

5 tablespoons margarine, divided
2 large onions, sliced thin
1 pound beef liver
3 tablespoons lemon juice
½ cup sesame seeds

Melt 3 tablespoons margarine in a large skillet, add onions and cook slowly over medium-low heat, stirring occasionally, until soft and golden, about 20 minutes. Meanwhile, cut liver crosswise into 1-inch strips, cover with lemon juice and let stand for 10 minutes. Remove onions from skillet; add remaining 2 tablespoons margarine. Drain liver and dredge in sesame seeds. Sauté liver in margarine over medium-high heat until browned on all sides, about 3 to 5 minutes. Serve topped with onions. Serves 4.

Oven-Browned Potatoes

4 medium potatoes
¼ cup melted butter or margarine
¼ cup oil
Salt

Scrub potatoes well and cut as for french fries, about 1 inch thick. Dip potatoes in the combined butter and oil. Arrange in a single layer in a shallow baking pan and bake at 400° for 40 minutes or until lightly browned and puffy. Salt to taste. Serves 4.

Zucchini with Tomatoes

1 small onion, chopped
1 tablespoon oil
1 pound fresh zucchini, sliced
2 medium fresh tomatoes, coarsely chopped
Salt and pepper

Sauté onion in oil until transparent. Add zucchini and tomatoes and cook, covered, over medium heat until zucchini is tender, 10 to 15 minutes. Salt and pepper to taste. Serves 4.

QUILTING HINT: *Stored quilts should be wrapped in cotton sheeting and stored in a dark, cool, airy place. Dampness and plastic bags are real enemies of stored quilts.*

Fifty-four Forty or Fight

"Fifty-four Forty or Fight" was the slogan of expansionists in 1846, but a treaty with Great Britain set the northern border of the Oregon country at a different latitude. This was the hot issue of the time; the hottest thing in this menu is the oven temperature.

MENU
400-40 AND EAT
BROCCOLI WITH LEMON WEDGES
TABBOULI SALAD
PRESERVED ORANGE SLICES

400-40 *and Eat*

1 *package seasoned dressing mix*
1 *chicken, cut in serving pieces*
¼ *cup margarine, melted*

Preheat oven to 400°. Prepare 4 cups dressing according to package directions, or use your own favorite recipe. Spread dressing on bottom of a 9-by-13-inch baking dish. Place chicken, skin side up, on top of dressing and brush with margarine. Bake for 20 minutes, baste with remaining margarine and bake 20 minutes longer. Serves 4-6.

Tabbouli Salad

1 *cup bulgur wheat*
2 *cups boiling water*
½ *cup oil*
½ *cup lemon juice*
2 *teaspoons salt*
1 *teaspoon pepper*
¾ *cup chopped parsley*
3 *tablespoons chopped fresh mint or*
  2 *teaspoons dried mint, crumbled*
1 *bunch green onions with tops, finely chopped*
2 *tomatoes, seeded and diced*

Pour boiling water over wheat and let stand 1 hour. Drain, squeeze dry and return to bowl. Add remaining ingredients and mix well. Chill at least 2 hours. Serve on lettuce leaves. Serves 6.

Preserved Orange Slices

These can be made ahead and kept for several months.

2 *medium oranges*
2 *cups sugar*
1 *cup orange juice*

Wash and dry oranges. Cut into ¼-inch slices, discarding ends and seeds. In a saucepan, combine sugar and orange juice and boil, without stirring, to the soft-ball stage (238° on a candy thermometer). Add oranges, bring to a boil and simmer about 15 minutes. Oranges should be transparent and tender but still hold their shape. Pack in container, cover and refrigerate. This makes 3 cups. To serve, place 2 slices with a little of the syrup on each dessert plate; sprinkle with a little grated coconut or chopped nuts.

QUILTING HINT: *Quilt borders require long straight strips. Cut them from the fabric first, before patches and smaller pieces are cut.*

Rolling Pinwheel

Rolling Pinwheel is like the fireworks at the end of a Fourth of July display. If caution is not used when adding the chili powder, this tamale pie could produce fireworks.

MENU
TAMALE PIE

HOT FLAT BREAD

ORANGE-PEPPER SALAD

SUGAR DONUTS

Tamale Pie

1 pound ground beef
½ green pepper, chopped
½ onion, chopped
2 garlic cloves, minced
1 1-pound 8-ounce can tomatoes
2 tablespoons chili powder
½ teaspoon cayenne pepper
1 7-ounce bag corn chips
¾ cup cheddar cheese, grated

Sauté beef, peppers, onion and garlic together until meat is browned and vegetables are soft. Add tomatoes, chili powder and cayenne pepper, mix well and simmer for 10 minutes. In a casserole, put a layer of slightly crushed corn chips, then a layer of meat sauce; repeat, ending with a layer of corn chips. Top with grated cheese. Bake at 350° for 20 to 25 minutes or until cheese melts. Serves 4.

Hot Flat Bread

1 loaf unbaked frozen bread, thawed
1 teaspoon salt
3 tablespons oil
¼ teaspoon basil
2 tablespoons Parmesan cheese

Roll out bread to fit a 9½-by-13-inch rimmed baking pan. With thumb, poke holes in the dough 1 inch apart. Mix salt, oil and basil together and sprinkle over the bread. Dust with cheese. Let rise in a warm place about 30 minutes, or until double in size. Bake at 425° for 12 to 15 minutes. Cut into strips and serve hot. Makes 15 pieces.

Orange-Pepper Salad

3 oranges
1 small onion, chopped
1 green pepper, chopped
Lettuce leaves
Oil and vinegar dressing

Peel, slice and seed oranges. In a flat serving dish, arrange orange slices on lettuce leaves and sprinkle with chopped onion and pepper. Chill. Just before serving, pour dressing over salad. Serves 4.

QUILTING HINT: *Using quarter-inch graph paper to draft patterns makes adding the seam allowance accurate and easy — just move over one quarter-inch square.*

Compass

Compass is a fitting name for this complex quilt; one can imagine the captain charting his course with the compass rose (Nor' east by east) as he heads for the shrimping grounds.

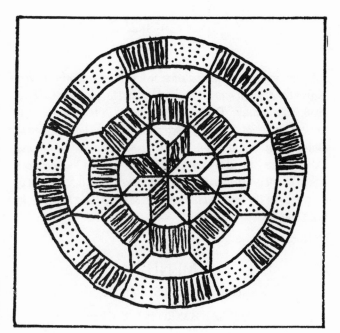

MENU
SWEET AND SOUR SHRIMP

HOT BUTTERED NOODLES

SLICED TOMATOES AND GREEN ONIONS

FRESH FRUIT IN SEASON

Sweet and Sour Shrimp

1 pound cooked and cleaned shrimp
¼ cup brown sugar
2 tablespoons cornstarch
¼ teaspoon salt
¼ cup wine vinegar
1 tablespoon soy sauce
1 2-pound can pineapple chunks, drained (reserve juice)
1 green pepper, chopped
2 small onions, chopped

In a saucepan mix brown sugar, cornstarch, salt, wine vinegar, soy sauce and juice from drained pineapple. Cook, stirring constantly, until thickened a little. Add green pepper, onion and pineapple chunks and cook briefly, 3 to 4 minutes. Remove from stove, add shrimp and let stand 10 minutes. Reheat just before serving, stirring carefully so it doesn't burn. Serves 4.

Sliced Tomatoes and Green Onions

Wash and slice tomatoes, about one per person. Sprinkle with salt, pepper, a pinch of sugar, some sliced green onions and oil and vinegar dressing.

COOKING HINT: A *few fresh celery leaves added to the cooking water will reduce the odor of boiling shrimp.*

Idaho

Idaho, with its curved patches, would be a daylight, rather than a candlelight quilt — and not the first to be attempted by a beginning quilter. Before electric lights, the quilter often worked on two at once — a fancy quilt when the light was good and a plain one at night. Baking potatoes is for beginning cooks; it is as easy as boiling water. Just remember that potatoes baked in foil get steamed rather than baked, and there's a lot of difference in the taste. Idaho potatoes seem to have the edge in taste, too.

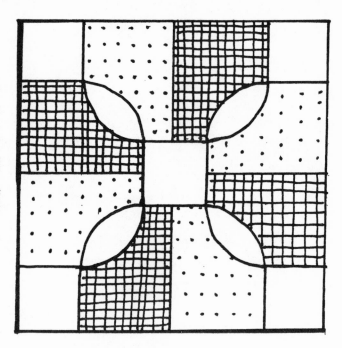

MENU

HAMBURGER SURPRISE

SPECIAL BAKED POTATOES

CRISP VEGETABLE PLATE

CARROT CAKE

Hamburger Surprise

½ medium onion, chopped fine
¼ pound mushrooms, sliced
2 tablespoons oil
1 pound ground beef
2 eggs
1 tablespoon flour
1 teaspoon salt
Dash of pepper
¼ cup ketchup
4 slices bacon

Sauté onions and mushrooms in oil until golden. Mix meat, eggs, flour, salt, pepper and ketchup together and beat until fluffy, about 5 minutes. Form into 8 thin patties. Spread sautéed onions and mushrooms on 4 patties, place remaining 4 on top and pinch edges tightly together. Wrap a strip of bacon around the outside edge of each patty and fasten with a toothpick. Fry in a hot, greased skillet. The patties can be prepared ahead, refrigerated and fried at the last minute. Serves 4.

Special Baked Potatoes

4 baking potatoes
1 teaspoon salt
Pepper to taste
¼ cup hot milk
2 tablespoons butter
½ cup grated cheddar cheese
Paprika

Select four uniform potatoes. Scrub well, pierce and bake at 425° for 50 minutes. Cut in half lengthwise, scoop out the insides, mix with salt, pepper, milk and butter. Beat until creamy. Refill the shells and sprinkle with cheese and paprika. Bake at 350° about 5 to 10 minutes. Serves 4.

QUILTING HINT: *Transparent rulers, 6 and 18 inches long, are invaluable tools for quilters.*

Chinese Ten-Thousand Perfections

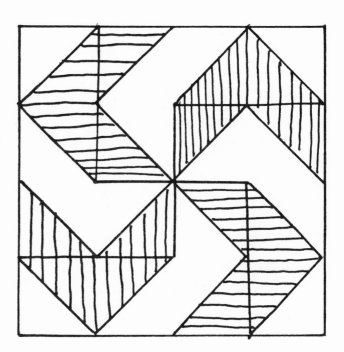

Chinese Ten-Thousand Perfections is a design that has seemingly ten thousand unusual names — Swastika; Heart's Seal; Ax of Thor; The Pure Symbol of the Right Doctrine; Favorite of the Peruvians; Mound Builders and more. This is a meal with at least five perfections — the other nine thousand, nine hundred and ninety-five might be just too much.

MENU
PERFECT PORK CHOPS

CHINESE SALAD

STEAMED RICE

CHILLED MANDARIN ORANGES

FORTUNE COOKIES

Perfect Pork Chops

6 pork chops
1 teaspoon ginger
1 teaspoon salt
½ teaspoon pepper
1 teaspoon paprika
¼ cup flour
2 tablespoons shortening
1 cup pineapple juice
2 tablespoons vinegar
3 tablespoons brown sugar

Combine seasonings with flour. Dredge chops in flour and brown in hot shortening. Transfer to an ovenproof dish. Combine pineapple juice, vinegar and brown sugar and pour over chops. Bake at 300° for 1 hour. More juice may be added if chops become dry. Serves 3-6.

Chinese Salad

2 cups bean sprouts, fresh or canned
½ cup diced celery
1 cucumber, sliced thin
1 green pepper, minced
2 tomatoes, cut in small cubes
Soy sauce
½ cup French dressing
Mayonnaise
Minced chives

If using canned bean sprouts, rinse and drain. Combine all vegetables. Add a few drops soy sauce to French dressing and pour over vegetables. Toss well and refrigerate for 1 hour. To serve, drain off excess dressing and pass mayonnaise and chives for topping. Serves 6.

Fortune Cookies

Write your own fortunes and place them under the family's favorite cookies.

COOKING HINT: No need to consult the package when cooking rice; just use twice as much liquid as dry rice. The liquid may be meat stock, bouillon cubes dissolved in hot water or just water.

Honey Bee

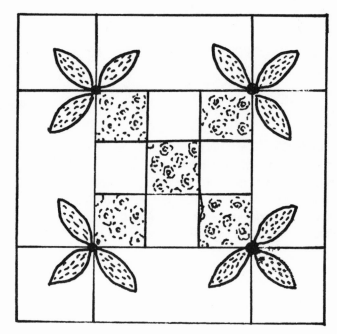

Honey Bee is a pretty pattern, just right for a young girl's room if you make it in pastel spring colors. And Honey Sauce is just the thing for any cake you choose to top off this meal.

MENU
BEEF BRISKET

CHEESY CORN BREAD MUFFINS

SLICED BEETS AND COTTAGE CHEESE ON LETTUCE

POUND CAKE WITH HONEY SAUCE

Beef Brisket

This is best prepared a day in advance.

1 4-to-5-pound beef brisket
1½ teaspoons seasoned salt
2 teaspoons pepper
2 teaspoons celery salt
1 teaspoon garlic salt
1-2 teaspoons Worcestershire sauce

Make a paste of seasonings and Worcestershire sauce and rub into all sides of brisket. Wrap tightly in foil and bake 8 hours at 225°. Refrigerate overnight in its juices. Remove hardened fat. Slice and reheat in juices. Serves 4.

Cheesy Corn Bread Muffins

1 cup all-purpose flour
¼ cup sugar
3 teaspoons baking powder
½ teaspoon salt
¾ cup corn meal
1 cup milk
¼ cup cooking oil
1 egg, well beaten
3 ounces sharp cheese, grated

Sift together flour, sugar, baking powder and salt. Stir in corn meal. Add milk, oil, egg and cheese; stir just until moist. Fill 12 well-greased muffin-pan cups ⅔ full. Bake at 425° for 20 to 25 minutes.

Honey Sauce

½ pint whipping cream
½ cup honey
1 teaspoon lemon juice

Beat cream until thick, add honey and lemon juice and continue beating until blended. Spoon sauce over slices of homemade or purchased pound cake.

QUILTING HINT: Allow an additional 12 to 14 inches on all four sides for the overhang of a quilt to be used with a dust ruffle.

Duck Paddle

Duck Paddle recreates the impressions of webbed feet in the soft earth beside the farm pond. Those farm ducklings probably never became a dish as elegant and sophisticated — and surprisingly easy to prepare — as our Duckling with Orange Sauce.

MENU

DUCKLING WITH ORANGE SAUCE

BAKED RATATOUILLE

PEACH MELBA

Duckling with Orange Sauce

1 duckling, about 4-6 pounds
2 tablespoons sugar
1 tablespoon cornstarch
1 teaspoon powdered ginger
½ teaspoon salt
1½ cups orange juice
2 teaspoons lemon rind
⅔ cup hot water
1 orange, sectioned

Rinse duck inside and out with cold water. Cut in quarters and dry. Place skin side up on a rack in a shallow roasting pan. Roast, uncovered, at 350° for 2 hours.

To make sauce: blend sugar, cornstarch, ginger and salt in saucepan. Stir in orange juice and lemon rind. Cook, stirring constantly, until mixture thickens and comes to a boil. When duck is done, put it into an ovenproof serving dish. Pour off all fat from pan. Add hot water to pan to dissolve brown particles. Add pan liquid to orange sauce. Pour heated sauce over duck quarters and arrange orange sections around duck. Reheat at 350° for 10 to 15 minutes or until hot. Serves 4.

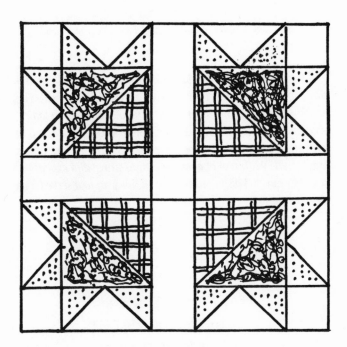

Baked Ratatouille

1 small eggplant, peeled and cubed
2 green peppers, sliced
3 tomatoes, seeded and diced
2 zucchini, sliced
1 large onion, chopped
2 cloves garlic, crushed
¼ cup olive oil
Salt and pepper to taste

Place vegetables in a 4-quart casserole. Season with salt and pepper. Add garlic and olive oil. Cover. Bake at 350° for 30 to 40 minutes or until vegetables are tender. May be served hot or cold. Serves 4-6.

Peach Melba

1 1-pound can peach halves, drained
1 pint vanilla ice cream
1 jar raspberry sauce or raspberry preserves

Place one peach half in each of 4 serving dishes. Place a scoop of ice cream on each peach half and top with raspberry sauce or preserves. Serves 4.

QUILTING HINT: Stored quilts should be rolled, not folded. If this isn't possible, change the folds from time to time from quarters to thirds.

Star and Crescent

Star and Crescent is an old Pennsylvania Dutch pattern, difficult to make because of the curved pieces in the block. The stitching was no problem for the Mennonite and Amish ladies, who excelled at such arduous tasks. There's nothing arduous to preparing Chickalone — and it's as new as Star and Crescent is traditional. With real abalone becoming scarce and expensive, a California chef disguised chicken in this way and served it as the real thing.

MENU

CHICKALONE

PEAS WITH PEARL ONIONS

SOUTHERN SPOON BREAD

BUTTERSCOTCH SUNDAES

Chickalone

To be prepared a day ahead.

2 chicken breasts, halved
1 small bottle clam juice
Seasoned bread crumbs
Butter and vegetable oil

Bone and skin the chicken breasts; place between sheets of plastic wrap and pound thin with the flat side of a cleaver or with a bottle. Place chicken in a shallow dish, cover with clam juice and marinate, covered, in refrigerator overnight. In a heavy skillet, heat to sizzling enough butter and oil (half each) to cover the bottom of the pan. Coat chicken breasts, lifted directly from the clam juice, with seasoned crumbs. Brown quickly on each side, about 2 minutes each. Remove to serving platter and keep warm. Serves 4.

Southern Spoon Bread

2 cups water
½ teaspoon salt
2 tablespoons cooking oil
1 cup yellow corn meal
3 eggs, separated
1 cup milk
1 teaspoon baking powder

Bring water to boil in 2-quart heavy saucepan. Add salt and oil. Slowly add cornmeal, stirring constantly to prevent lumps. Cook until thick, about 1 minute. Remove from heat and cool 10 minutes. Beat egg yolks one at a time into the corn meal. Add milk and mix thoroughly. Beat egg whites until frothy, add baking powder and beat until stiff. Fold lightly but thoroughly into corn meal mixture. Turn into a 6-cup greased casserole and bake at 325° for 1 to 1¼ hours. Spoon out and serve hot with lots of butter. Serves 6.

COOKING HINT: Sixteen tablespoons equal one cup.

Sugarloaf

Sugarloaf reminds us that refined sugar was once molded into cone shapes, and there are hills and mountains all over the country with this name. Our tomato-cheese pie is similar to a quiche — and there are as many kinds of quiche as there are sugarloaf mountains.

MENU
TOMATO-CHEESE PIE

LEMON-BUTTERED BROCCOLI

CRANBERRY CRUNCH

Tomato-Cheese Pie

2 cups fresh bread crumbs
¼ cup melted margarine
1 cup grated cheddar cheese, divided
1 1-pound can tomatoes
1 tablespoon cornstarch
2 teaspoons instant onion
½ teaspoon salt
1 teaspoon sugar
½ teaspoon crushed basil
2 eggs
¾ cup milk

Combine crumbs, margarine and ¼ cup cheese. Press into a 9-inch pie plate. Bake at 400° for 10 minutes or until lightly browned. Cool. Drain liquid from tomatoes into saucepan. Blend in cornstarch. Add onion, salt, sugar and basil; cook, stirring constantly, until thickened. Slice tomatoes and arrange in pie shell. Pour thickened liquid over tomatoes. Beat eggs, milk and rest of cheese together. Pour over top of pie. Bake at 375° for 40 minutes. Cool 10 minutes before slicing. Slice in pie-shaped wedges. Serves 4-6.

Lemon-Buttered Broccoli

2 10-ounce packages frozen broccoli spears
1 tablespoon lemon juice
3 tablespoons margarine, melted

Cook broccoli according to package directions. Combine lemon juice and margarine and pour over broccoli. Serve hot. Serves 6.

Cranberry Crunch

1 cup raw rolled oats
½ cup flour
1 cup brown sugar
½ cup (¼ pound) margarine
1 can cranberry sauce, jellied or whole berry
Vanilla ice cream

Mix oats, flour and brown sugar together. Cut in margarine until crumbly. Place half of the mixture in a greased 8-by-8-inch baking dish. Cover with cranberry sauce, then top with rest of mixture. Bake at 375° for 30 minutes or until the top is browned. Serve warm in squares topped with vanilla ice cream. Serves 6-8.

QUILTING HINT: *Tag one pair of scissors for cutting fabric only. Cutting paper will dull them.*

Kaleidoscope

Kaleidoscope really looks like the image you see through one! The colors and shapes in this salad may seem kaleidoscopic, too, with the varied colors and shapes of oranges, spinach and peanuts.

MENU

BAKED DRUMSTICKS

BRUSSELS SPROUTS

ORANGE-SPINACH SALAD WITH PEANUTS

DROP SUGAR COOKIES (page 54)

Baked Drumsticks

6-8 chicken drumsticks
Salt
Paprika
2 tablespoons margarine, melted
1 tablespoon lemon juice
½ teaspoon dried tarragon

Line a shallow baking dish with aluminum foil. Season drumsticks with salt and paprika. Combine margarine, lemon juice and tarragon. Brush drumsticks with half the mixture and bake at 375° for 30 minutes. Turn drumsticks, brush with remaining margarine and lemon juice and bake 15 minutes longer. Serves 4.

Brussels Sprouts

10-12 ounces fresh brussels sprouts
1 onion, chopped
1 tablespoon cooking oil
1 8-ounce can tomato purée
Salt and pepper

Remove discolored leaves from sprouts. Wash well and cut an X in the stem end. Steam until just tender, about 10 minutes. Sauté onion in oil, add tomato purée and bring to a boil. Add sprouts, season with salt and pepper and heat until piping hot. Serves 4.

Orange-Spinach Salad with Peanuts

1 11-ounce can mandarin oranges
½ bunch spinach
Oil and vinegar dressing
½ cup chopped peanuts

Drain oranges thoroughly. Wash spinach, discard stems and pat dry. Tear into bite-sized pieces and toss with dressing. Add oranges and peanuts just before serving. Serves 4.

QUILTING HINT: *Toss scraps and long narrow strips of cloth into a plastic bag to make a string quilt or spider-web blocks later.*

Blazing Star

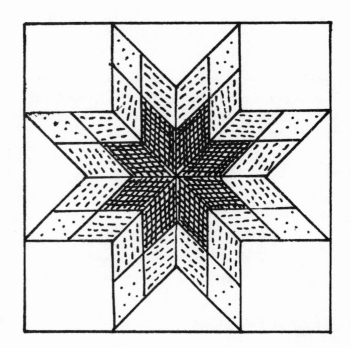

Blazing Star is one of the many, many stars made from different-colored diamond patches; this one is especially effective. These ham balls are one of the many, many ways to use leftover ham that may be more delicious than the original.

MENU

HAM BALLS WITH MUSTARD SAUCE

GLAZED SWEET POTATOES

SAVORY CABBAGE

LEMON SHERBET

Ham Balls with Mustard Sauce

1 pound ground ham
1 pound ground pork
½ cup milk
2 eggs
½ cup cornflake crumbs or cracker crumbs
¼ cup finely chopped onion
1 teaspoon prepared mustard
⅛ teaspoon pepper

Combine all ingredients and mix well. Shape into 24 balls. Place on greased baking pan. Bake at 350° for 1 hour. Top with dill mustard sauce. Serves 6.

Dill Mustard Sauce

2 tablespoons margarine
2 tablespoons flour
½ teaspoon salt
1 cup milk
½ cup sour cream
1 tablespoon prepared Dijon mustard
¼ teaspoon dried dill weed

Melt margarine; stir in flour and salt. Add milk; cook, stirring constantly, until smooth and thickened. Stir in sour cream, mustard and dill. Heat slowly to serving temperature but do not boil. Serve over ham balls.

Savory Cabbage

1 medium head cabbage
½ teaspoon salt
½ teaspoon sugar
¼ cup dried onion flakes
2 tablespoons margarine
1 tablespoon lemon juice
½ teaspoon caraway seeds (optional)

Shred cabbage. Place in a saucepan with 1 inch boiling water, salt, sugar and onion flakes. Boil uncovered 5 minutes; cover and cook until cabbage is just tender, about 3 minutes more. Drain if necessary. Toss with salt and pepper to taste, margarine, lemon juice and caraway seeds. Serves 6.

QUILTING HINT: It is tempting to tear long strips of cloth for quilt borders, but the distortion and fringe that often result usually must be evened off with scissors, so little time is saved. It is neater and cleaner to cut strips in the first place.

Streaks of Lightning

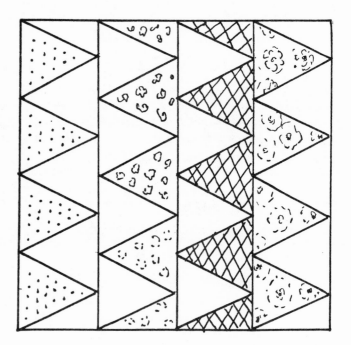

Streaks of Lightning is a simple pattern of repeated triangles, a good pattern for using up small scraps of cloth. The family will never believe that this meal was simple to put together—they'll think the cook had to be a streak of lightning.

MENU

SHRIMP AND RICE CASSEROLE

BAKED TOMATOES (page 22)

AVOCADO AND SPINACH SALAD

CHOCOLATE CAKE (FROM BAKERY OR FREEZER)

Shrimp and Rice Casserole

1 cup raw rice
1½ cups canned or cooked fresh shrimp
¼ cup green onions, minced
1 tablespoon margarine
½ cup chicken bouillon
1 10-ounce package frozen green peas, partially thawed
Salt and pepper to taste
1 garlic clove, minced
1 tablespoon cornstarch
¼ cup water
½ cup grated Parmesan cheese
¼ cup dry bread crumbs
Butter

Cook rice according to directions on package. Butter a casserole generously. Spread cooked rice over bottom of casserole. In a skillet, sauté shrimp and green onions in margarine for 4 minutes. Add chicken bouillon, peas, salt, pepper and garlic. Dissolve cornstarch in water. Stir into shrimp mixture and simmer until thickened slightly. Pour over rice in casserole. Top with cheese and bread crumbs and dot with butter. Heat at 325° for 30 minutes. Serves 6.

Avocado and Spinach Salad

1 bunch fresh spinach
1 small Bermuda onion, chopped fine
1 hard-boiled egg, chopped fine
1 avocado, sliced

Dressing

1 cup oil
¼ cup sugar
⅓ cup vinegar
½ teaspoon dry mustard
½ teaspoon salt

Wash and dry spinach thoroughly. Discard stems and coarse leaves. Tear into bite-sized pieces and combine with onion and egg. Mix dressing ingredients together and beat until sugar dissolves and dressing thickens slightly. Just before serving, add avocado and toss with dressing. Serves 6.

QUILTING HINT: *Crazy quilts may be made of various fabrics—silk, velvet, satin, wool—all in the same quilt. The embroidery along the seam lines is the unifying element.*

King's Crown

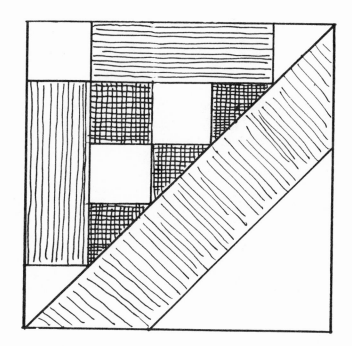

King's Crown: *Since the early settlers' lives were largely centered around their religious beliefs, some think this pattern was so called because of the hymn "Coronation": "Bring forth the royal diadem and crown him Lord of all." At any rate, this menu will be royal fare, for king or vassal.*

MENU

PEACHY PORK CHOPS WITH SAUERKRAUT

ITALIAN GREEN BEANS AND WATER CHESTNUTS

APPLE AND CELERY SALAD

FROZEN CHEESECAKE

Peachy Pork Chops with Sauerkraut

4 lean loin pork chops, cut ¾-inch thick
Salt and pepper to taste
1 1-pound can sliced peaches, drained (reserve 3 tablespoons syrup)
3 tablespoons ketchup
1 1-pound can Bavarian style saukerkraut, drained

In a large skillet, brown pork chops lightly on both sides. Season with salt and pepper. Add peach syrup, ketchup and sauerkraut. Cover and cook 45 to 60 minutes over low heat until chops are fork-tender. Add peach slices and heat through. Serves 4.

Italian Green Beans and Water Chestnuts

1 9-ounce package frozen Italian green beans
½ cup chicken bouillon
⅓ cup sliced water chestnuts
1 tablespoon margarine

Prepare green beans according to package directions, but substitute chicken bouillon for the water. When cooked, drain and add water chestnuts and margarine. Reheat. Serves 4.

Apple and Celery Salad

1 cup diced celery
1 cup diced, unpeeled apple
½ cup broken walnut meats
2 teaspoons lemon juice
½ cup mayonnaise

Combine all ingredients. Toss lightly and serve on lettuce leaves. Serves 4.

QUILTING HINT: *If the thought of making a large quilt is overwhelming, start with a pillow top or a single quilt block to be used as a skirt pocket or a bag decoration.*

Prickly Pear

Prickly Pear is aptly named for the fruit of a member of the cactus family, with all the pointed triangles resembling thorns. The avocado is a fruit of a member of the laurel family; the peach is from a tree in the rose family. We could have called for candied, pickled prickly pears for dessert.

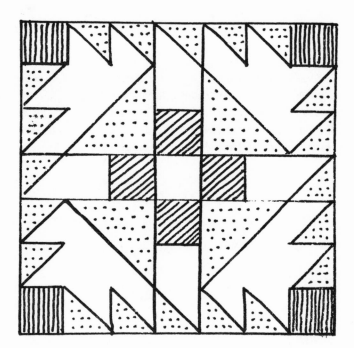

MENU

CHEF'S SEAFOOD SALAD

HERBED MUFFINS

PEACH PIE

Chef's Seafood Salad

2 ripe avocados
1 pound flaked cooked crab meat or small shrimp
Mayonnaise
Lettuce
4 hard-boiled eggs, sliced
Lemon wedges

Halve and peel avocados. Mix seafood with just enough mayonnaise to bind together. On individual serving plates, place half an avocado on a bed of shredded lettuce, mound seafood in center, garnish with egg slices and a lemon wedge. Pass dressing in separate bowl. Serves 4.

Dressing

1 cup mayonnaise
¾ cup chili sauce
½ teaspoon lemon juice
½ teaspoon horseradish
⅛ cup chopped sour pickles
¼ teaspoon Worcestershire sauce

Mix all ingredients together well. Chill until ready to serve. Makes about 2 cups.

Herbed Muffins

2 tablespoons dried herbs—chives, parsley and oregano or basil
¼ cup butter
4 English muffins

Mix herbs with butter. Split muffins and spread generously with butter. Toast in broiler, watching carefully so they don't burn. Serves 4.

Peach Pie

1 9-inch graham cracker pie crust, baked
5 fresh peaches, peeled and sliced
½ pint heavy cream, whipped

Fill baked pie crust with layers of peaches and whipped cream. Chill until ready to serve. Serves 4-6.

COOKING HINT: Store eggs with the small end down to keep the yolks centered.

Cube Work

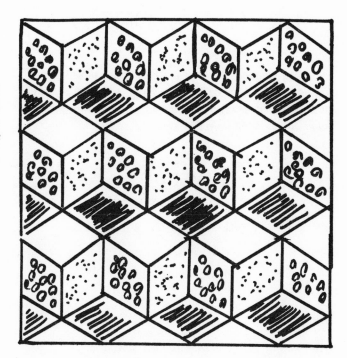

Cube Work is a pattern of diamonds especially popular in early New England, also known as Baby Blocks. Properly pieced (and it is not an easy pattern because of all the points to be gotten together neatly), it becomes an eye-fooling field of cubes. The cubes of beef fillet in this fondue become a melt-in-the-mouth delicacy.

MENU
BEEF FONDUE WITH SAUCES

BOILED OR BAKED POTATOES

GREEN SALAD

COFFEE DELIGHT

Beef Fondue

2 pounds filet of beef
1 cup salad oil
1 cup butter
Sauces

Cut beef in bite-sized pieces (about 1-inch cubes) and pile into a bowl. In a fondue pot or electric frying pan, heat oil and butter to bubbling. Give each guest a fondue fork and let each cook beef according to taste—about 10 seconds for rare, 30 seconds for well done. Dip cooked meat into sauces of choice. Serves 6.

Sour Cream and Horseradish Sauce

¾ cup sour cream
1 tablespoon prepared horseradish
Salt to taste

Put all ingredients in a bowl and mix well.

Tomato Sauce

1 cup ketchup
1 small carrot, finely grated
1 teaspoon Tabasco sauce
2 teaspoons Worcestershire sauce
2 tablespoons vinegar
2 tablespoons butter

Combine all ingredients in a saucepan and simmer for 15 minutes. Reheat just before serving and serve warm.

Mustard Sauce

¼ cup prepared mustard
¼ cup mayonnaise
1 garlic clove, minced
¼ teaspoon Tabasco sauce

Combine ingredients, mix and refrigerate until ready to serve.

Coffee Delight

1 cup miniature marshmallows
1 cup hot, strong coffee
½ pint whipping cream

In a bowl, combine marshmallows and coffee and let stand until cool. Whip cream until stiff, fold in marshmallows and pour into a 2-quart dish. Freeze until firm. This dessert keeps well in freezer and can be made ahead. Serves 6–8.

COOKING HINT: Freeze cubes of coffee to cool iced coffee. The iced coffee will stay good and strong, and you won't have to start with acid, too-strong coffee.

Darting Minnows

Darting Minnows could be a school of fish shooting in all directions in the water, or it could well suggest a catch of shrimp milling about in the net of a trawler that was gathering the main ingredient of this Shrimp Foo Yung.

MENU

SHRIMP FOO YUNG

MAKE-AHEAD PEA SALAD

RICE

PEARS CHANTILLY

Shrimp Foo Yung

1 cup shrimp, fresh cooked or canned, shredded
1 cup finely-chopped onions
¼ cup thinly-sliced water chestnuts (bean sprouts may be used instead)
½ cup chopped mushrooms
5 eggs
2 teaspoons soy sauce
Cooking oil

Stir together the shredded shrimp, onions, water chestnuts or bean sprouts, mushrooms, eggs and soy sauce. Heat a small amount of oil on a griddle or frying pan. Drop shrimp mixture by spoonfuls into oil. When brown on one side, turn over and brown other side. Serves 4.

Make-Ahead Pea Salad

Prepare this in the early morning or the day before.

2 10-ounce packages frozen peas
½ to 1 pound fresh mushrooms, sliced
3 tablespoons chopped chives
2 5-ounce cans water chestnuts, drained and sliced
½ cup oil and vinegar dressing

Cook peas according to package directions. Combine with remaining ingredients, toss with dressing and marinate all day or overnight in the refrigerator. Serves 8.

Pears Chantilly

¼ cup whipping cream, beaten until stiff
⅓ cup chopped nutmeats
½ tablespoon sugar
¼ teaspoon vanilla
6 canned pear halves

Combine stiffly beaten cream, nuts, sugar, and vanilla. Pile lightly into hollows of chilled pear halves. Serves 4–6.

QUILTING HINT: A large hoop works well for quilting and is portable.

Turkey Tracks

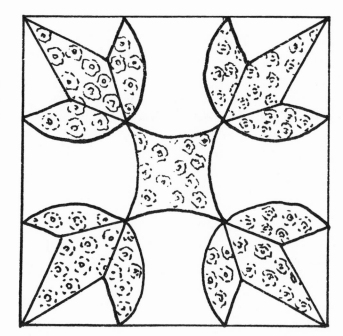

Turkey Tracks could have been made by a turkey that didn't know which direction to go, since the tracks point to the four winds. The turkey wandered far enough to get a Chinese flavor in this Sweet and Sour Turkey.

MENU
SWEET AND SOUR TURKEY
BARLEY PILAF
CHOCOLATE CAKE

Sweet and Sour Turkey

2 cups cubed, cooked turkey (use leftover turkey meat, or poach frozen turkey breast or thigh)
1 onion, sliced thin
2 ribs celery, sliced diagonally
1 green pepper, diced
3 tablespoons oil
¼ cup soy sauce
¼ cup vinegar
2 tablespoons brown sugar
4 teaspoons cornstarch
1 10-ounce can sliced peaches, drained (reserve syrup)

Sauté onion, celery and green pepper in oil for 5 minutes. Mix soy sauce, vinegar, brown sugar, cornstarch and reserved peach syrup. Stir into vegetables and cook, stirring, until thickened. Add turkey and peach slices and heat through. Serves 4–6.

Barley Pilaf

4 tablespoons margarine, divided
¼ pound mushrooms, sliced
1 medium onion, chopped
1 cup pearl barley
2 cups rich chicken stock or 3 chicken bouillon cubes dissolved in 2 cups boiling water

Heat 2 tablespoons margarine in heavy skillet and cook mushrooms gently. Lift out and cook onions until wilted. Add remaining margarine, pour in barley and cook slowly, turning frequently, until beautifully brown. Add mushrooms and chicken stock to barley. Cover tightly. Bake at 350° for 30 minutes. Fluff with fork and add more stock if barley looks dry. Re-cover and bake 20 minutes longer. Taste test. If softer barley is desired, bake about 10 minutes more. Serves 4.

Chocolate Cake

A cake from your favorite bakery or a frozen one will be easy on the cook and please the family.

QUILTING HINT: Use a 16-inch pillow form for a 15-inch pillow top. The tight fit will help avoid floppy corners.

Cherry Basket

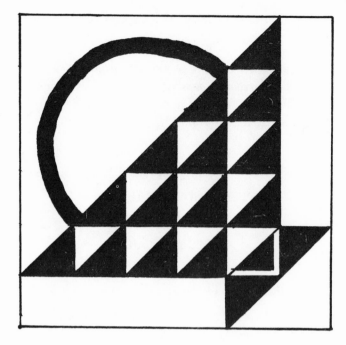

Baskets have long been favorites for quilt patterns, and this Cherry Basket is a fine example—it dates from the early nineteenth century at least. In honor of the quilt, finish this meal off with Cherry Basket Cookies.

MENU
CRUNCHY BAKED HAM SALAD

BISCUITS

CONFETTI COTTAGE CHEESE

CHERRY BASKET COOKIES

Crunchy Baked Ham Salad

3 cups diced cooked ham
1 cup diced celery
½ cup chopped stuffed green olives
2 hard cooked eggs, diced
½ cup chopped onion
1 tablespoon lemon juice
1 tablespoon prepared mustard
Dash of pepper
¾ cup mayonnaise
1 cup crushed potato chips

Combine all ingredients except potato chips. Spoon into a buttered casserole and top with crushed chips. Bake at 400° for 25 minutes. Serves 6.

Confetti Cottage Cheese

2 pints small curd cottage cheese
1 4-ounce can green chiles, seeded and chopped
¼ cup green onion, thinly sliced
½ teaspoon dill weed
Salt and pepper to taste

Mix all ingredients together, cover and chill for 1 hour. Serves 6.

Cherry Basket Cookies

1 cup butter
1 cup powdered sugar
¼ teaspoon salt
½ teaspoon vanilla
2 cups flour
1 8-ounce jar maraschino cherries, drained and chopped
½ cup nuts

Cream butter, add sugar and continue creaming until well blended. Stir in salt, vanilla, flour, cherries and nuts. Chill well. Shape into small balls and place on greased cookie sheets. Bake at 275° for 30 minutes or until lightly colored. Makes 4 to 5 dozen cookies.

COOKING HINT: For baking, 7/8 cup of all-purpose flour equals one cup of cake flour.

Hearts and Gizzards

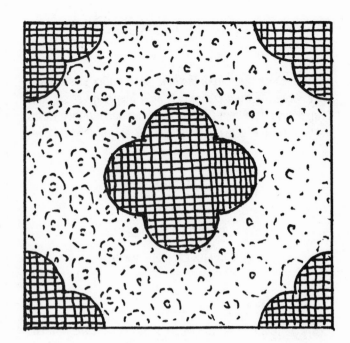

Hearts and Gizzards is an over-all design traditionally made in red and white. When you make Chicken Royal, save the hearts, gizzards and bones for soup.

MENU

CHICKEN ROYAL

RICE

BROCCOLI WITH LEMON

FRESH CRANBERRY-ORANGE RELISH

FROZEN YOGURT

Chicken Royal

1 4-ounce package chipped beef
6 chicken breasts, boned and skinned
6 slices bacon
1 10¾-ounce can cream of mushroom soup
½ pint sour cream

With scissors, cut up chipped beef and scatter over bottom of a small roasting pan. Wrap each chicken breast in bacon and place on top of beef. Combine mushroom soup and sour cream, pour over chicken breasts and bake, covered, at 275° for 2½ hours. Serves 6.

Fresh Cranberry-Orange Relish

2 cups cranberries
1 small orange, quartered
¾ cup sugar

Grind cranberries with orange, skin and all, or chop in blender. Mix with sugar and let stand a few hours before serving.

COOKING HINT: *For drier rice, at the end of 20 minutes' cooking, remove cover and leave over heat for a few minutes, tossing with a fork.*

Churn Dash

Churn Dash dates from the time when butter was made at home, from the thick cream that most homes never see now. Clam fritters date from the time when we dug our own clams, first finding them with our bare toes. Oh, for the good old days!

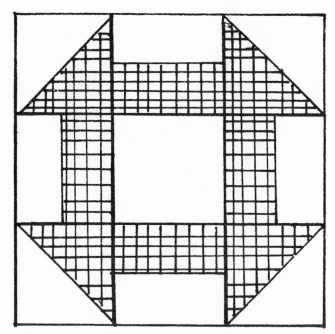

MENU

CLAM FRITTERS

FRIED TOMATOES

GEE WHIZ GINGER WHIP

Clam Fritters

2 cups minced clams, drained, or 3 6½-ounce cans minced
   clams
2 eggs, separated
1 cup fine dry bread crumbs
½ tablespoon each chopped fresh chives and fresh parsley
½ teaspoon salt
About ⅓ cup milk
Butter

Combine clams with well-beaten egg yolks, bread crumbs, chives, parsley and salt. Add just enough milk to make a heavy batter. Whip egg whites until stiff and fold carefully into clam mixture. Drop batter from a tablespoon onto a skillet or griddle containing a little heated butter. Fry fritters until golden on both sides. Serves 4–6.

Fried Tomatoes

6 medium-sized firm tomatoes
Flour
2 tablespoons margarine
1 tablespoon sugar
1 teaspoon salt
Dash of pepper
½ cup light cream

Cut unpeeled tomatoes in ½-inch thick slices; dredge in flour. Melt margarine in skillet and fry tomato slices over low heat until brown. Sprinkle with sugar, salt and pepper. With a pancake turner, lift onto warm serving dish. Blend cream into skillet drippings, stirring until smooth. Pour over tomatoes and serve at once. Serves 6.

Gee Whiz Ginger Whip

2 cups applesauce
¼ teaspoon ground cinnamon
1 stiffly beaten egg white
1 cup heavy cream
2 tablespoons sugar
¼ teaspoon ground ginger
Crystallized ginger

Mix applesauce with cinnamon and fold into beaten egg white. Whip cream with sugar and ground ginger and fold into applesauce mixture. Chill. Sprinkle with finely chopped crystallized ginger just before serving. Serves 6.

COOKING HINT: Always add a little sugar when cooking tomatoes to bring out the flavor.

Ice Cream Cone

Ice Cream Cone was first made by a professional quilter to help celebrate National Dairy Week—proving that the reasons for creating or naming quilt patterns are many. No one needs a reason to enjoy this meal. It's just right for the end of a warm day.

MENU
CREAM OF POTATO SOUP

BRAIDED SANDWICH LOAF

DILLY BEANS

ICE CREAM CONES

Cream of Potato Soup

5 cups thinly sliced potatoes
1 medium onion, sliced
1 teaspoon salt
3 tablespoons butter
1⅔ cups evaporated milk
1 cup water
1 tablespoon fresh parsley, finely chopped

Put potatoes and onion in a 3-quart saucepan and barely cover with water. Add salt, cover and bring to a boil. Lower heat and cook until potatoes are tender, about 20 minutes. Remove from heat and mash potatoes in their liquid. Add butter, milk and water. More milk may be added if necessary. Keep hot but not boiling. Adjust seasonings. Ladle into warmed soup cups and sprinkle with parsley. Serves 8-10.

Braided Sandwich Loaf

1 large loaf braided bread
1 cup chopped ripe olives
1 to 2 cups grated sharp cheese
6 fresh mushrooms, sliced
Mayonnaise
24 slices boiled ham or bologna
3 tomatoes, sliced

Slice bread in half lengthwise. Mix olives, cheese and mushrooms together and bind with a little mayonnaise. Spread mixture over bottom; layer ham and tomatoes. Cover with top half of loaf. Wrap tightly in foil and heat at 400° for about 20 minutes. Serve hot. Slice into 12 servings.

Dilly Beans

Make this a day or two ahead.
½ cup vinegar
½ cup water
¼ cup sugar
1½ teaspoons dried dill weed
¼ teaspoon salt
2 1-pound cans Blue Lake whole string beans, drained

Combine first 5 ingredients and bring to a boil. Pour over string beans and marinate in refrigerator overnight, or for several days if possible. Serves 6.

QUILTING HINT: When you want to give a gift to someone very special, consider a quilt. "If you own a quilt made especially for you, it says 'someone loves you'." —Progressive Farmer, January, 1973.

Stonemason's Puzzle

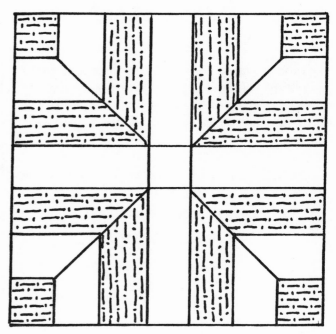

Stonemason's Puzzle does look somewhat like an ornamental assemblage of stones, and that may be the original source of the design. Since many of our masons were thought to come from Naples, let's dedicate this menu to them.

MENU
NEAPOLITAN HOTS

STUFFED CELERY

NEAPOLITAN ICE CREAM

Neapolitan Hots

8 hot Italian sausages
2 large onions, sliced thin
2 each red and green peppers, sliced thin
8 French sandwich rolls

Prick sausages with a fork. Cook for 15 minutes over medium heat in a large covered skillet to which 3 tablespoons water have been added. Uncover, push sausage to side of skillet, add onions and peppers and cook over low heat, stirring often, until onions are transparent and peppers limp. Slice rolls lengthwise. Put one sausage, together with a generous helping of onions and peppers, into each roll. Serve hot. Serves 4.

Stuffed Celery

4 stalks celery
1 3-ounce package cream cheese
¼ cup walnuts, chopped fine

Rinse and dry celery stalks. Mix cream cheese with walnuts and spread in center of celery. Cut into 1-inch pieces and chill until ready to serve. Serves 4.

QUILTING HINT: A tied quilt should be tied every 4 or 5 inches to be sure the inner filling does not shift.

102

Tree of Paradise

Tree of Paradise is one of the many trees depicted in quilt blocks. Pine Tree, Tree of Life, Live Oak Tree and Tree of Temptation are quite similar. From this last comes the applesauce in this tempting pork dish.

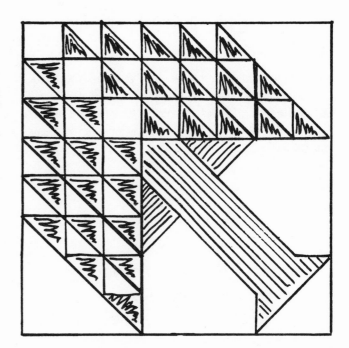

MENU
PORK CHOPS WITH APPLESAUCE

GREEN CHILE RICE

FRESH VEGETABLE PLATE

DATE-NUT TORTE

Pork Chops with Applesauce

6 large pork chops
Seasoned flour
1 tablespoon shortening
1 pint applesauce

Dredge pork chops in seasoned flour. In a heavy skillet, heat shortening and brown chops. Drain off excess fat. Pour applesauce over chops and cook over low heat for 45 minutes or until chops are tender. Serves 6.

Green Chile Rice

1 cup cooked rice
2 cups sour cream (reserve ½ cup for topping)
½ cup chopped green chiles
1 pound Romano or Parmesan cheese, grated
Salt and pepper to taste
½ chopped onion (optional)
2 tablespoons butter

Mix all ingredients together and spoon into a greased casserole. Top with remaining sour cream and dot with butter. Bake at 350° for 30 minutes. Serves 6.

Date-Nut Torte

4 eggs, separated
1 cup sugar
1 teaspoon baking powder
¼ cup soft bread crumbs
½ pound dates, cut in small pieces
½ pound walnut meats, chopped
Whipped cream

Beat egg yolks slightly; beat in sugar and baking powder; stir in bread crumbs, dates and nuts. Beat egg whites until stiff and fold into mixture. Put into a buttered baking dish, set in a pan of water and bake at 350° for 30 minutes. Serve cold with a dab of whipped cream.

COOKING HINT: Spice up canned applesauce with a little powdered cinnamon or cloves, or both.

English Ivy

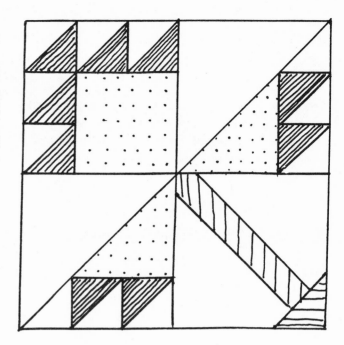

English Ivy, unlike most of the "leaf" patterns, is geometric, only suggesting the shape of the leaf. It is typical of older quilt patterns, though, in being composed of triangles and squares. Roast leg of lamb wouldn't be the same without the traditional suggestion of mint.

MENU
ROAST LAMB WITH MINT SAUCE

BRAISED ONIONS

TOSSED SALAD WITH CHOPPED EGG

HOT ROLLS

CINNAMON APPLESAUCE

Roast Lamb with Mint Sauce

1 6-pound leg of lamb
Salt and pepper
2 small onions, sliced

Rub lamb with salt and pepper, place on a rack in a shallow pan and cover with onion slices. Roast, uncovered, 18 minutes per pound for well done (175° on a meat thermometer), 12 minutes per pound for rare (140°). Remove to a warm platter and let stand 20 minutes before carving. Pass mint sauce in a bowl. Serves 8.

Mint Sauce

½ cup vinegar
1 tablespoon sugar
¼ cup chopped fresh mint leaves

Heat vinegar, add sugar and pour over mint leaves. Let stand about 45 minutes. Taste; if too strong, dilute with a little water. Makes ½ cup sauce.

Braised Onions

16 to 24 small white onions
⅔ cup beef broth
1 to 2 tablespoons sugar

Peel onions and cook in boiling water until tender but firm, about 10 to 15 minutes. Drain and place in a buttered casserole. Add beef broth, sprinkle lightly with sugar and bake at 350° until soft, about 20 minutes. Serves 8.

Cinnamon Applesauce

¼ teaspoon cinnamon
3 tablespoons sugar
3 tablespoons finely chopped walnuts or pecans
3 cups applesauce, canned or homemade

Mix cinnamon, sugar and nuts together. Spoon applesauce into stemmed glasses and sprinkle with cinnamon mixture. Serve with cookies, if desired. Serves 8.

QUILTING HINT: Outing flannel which has been washed and dried can be used as filler for crib quilts. It is lightweight and easy to quilt.

Kukui Nut

Kukui is a Hawaiian word meaning lamplight or torch. The tree the kukui nut grows on is also called the candlenut tree; the wood from the tree is used to make canoes, and oil from the nuts is burned for light. Use candles during this dinner for two, and think of drifting in a canoe on the calm blue Pacific.

MENU
FISH IN WINE

MASHED POTATOES

HEARTS OF PALM SALAD

MANGO MOUSSE

Fish in Wine

Waxed paper
1 tablespoon butter
1 medium onion, chopped
½ pound fresh mushrooms, sliced
2 pieces fillet of sole or other flat fish
¼ cup white wine

Cut a circle of waxed paper the same size as your frying pan. Cut a 1-inch hole in the center of the paper. Melt butter in the frying pan, add onions and half of the mushrooms. Cook about 2 minutes. Salt and pepper the fish, place fish on top of the onions, and add the remaining mushrooms and white wine. Lay waxed paper on top of fish, bring to a boil, and cover (leaving waxed paper in place) and cook 5 to 10 minutes or until fish is flaky. Serves 2.

Hearts of Palm Salad

1 can hearts of palm, chilled
Lettuce leaves
French dressing

Cut hearts of palm into lengthwise strips. Arrange on crisp lettuce leaves and serve with French dressing. Serves 2.

Mango Mousse

1 cup mashed ripe mangoes
1 cup pineapple juice
Juice of ½ lime
2 teaspoons sugar
1 pint heavy cream, whipped
Grated nutmeg

Combine mashed mangoes, pineapple juice, lime juice and sugar. Freeze mixture for 30 minutes. Beat mixture until it becomes softened and fold in whipped cream. Dust with grated nutmeg. Spoon into demitasse cups or small bowls and chill several hours.

QUILTING HINT: Like old silverware and old furniture, quilts develop a patina from many washings, years of use, and exposure to light.

Hawaiian Pineapple

The Hawaiian Pineapple is different from the several Colonial pineapple patterns, which are stylized. The Hawaiian Pineapple is realistic, typical of the elaborate appliquéd quilts originating in Hawaii. This meal isn't elaborate to prepare, but will bring aloha to your dining room.

MENU

HAM STEAK FROSTED WITH CAMEMBERT

HAWAIIAN SQUASH

HOT BUTTERED BEETS

THIN SLICED PUMPERNICKEL

COCONUT BARS

Ham Steak Frosted wtih Camembert

2 tablespoons margarine
Ham steak, 1 to 1½ inches thick
Ripe, creamy Camembert cheese at room temperature

In a large skillet, melt margarine to sizzling and sauté ham steak until lightly browned on both sides. Spread a thick coating of Camembert cheese on top. Serve as soon as cheese melts. Serves 6.

Hawaiian Squash

2 packages frozen yellow squash, thawed
1 cup pineapple chunks, drained
1 cup orange segments or canned Mandarin oranges, drained
3 tablespoons sour cream
2 tablespoons brown sugar
2 tablespoons chopped walnuts

Combine first 5 ingredients and mix gently. Bake in a buttered casserole at 350° for 20 minutes or until heated through. Sprinkle lightly with chopped walnuts before serving. Serves 6.

Coconut Bars

To be made ahead of time.

½ cup margarine
1½ cups brown sugar, divided
1 cup plus 1 tablespoon flour, divided
2 eggs
1 cup chopped walnuts
½ cup shredded coconut
1 teaspoon vanilla
Confectioner's sugar

Combine margarine, ½ cup brown sugar and 1 cup flour; cream until smooth. Spread in the bottom of an 8-inch-square pan and bake at 375° for 20 minutes. Beat eggs with 1 cup brown sugar until smooth. Add walnuts, coconut tossed with 1 tablespoon flour, and vanilla. Spread over the baked crust and bake another 20 minutes at 375°. Sprinkle with confectioner's sugar when cool, and cut into bars.

QUILTING HINT: *For sewing an accurate seam allowance, place a double strip of heavy tape on the throat plate of your sewing machine parallel to the presser foot and exactly ¼ inch from the needle. The fabric will ride along the tape as you sew.*

Index